A Guide for Special Education Bible Teaching-Reaching Ministry

A Place for Everyone

Athalene McNay

Convention Press
Nashville, Tennessee

This book is the text for Course Numbers LS-0104, LS-0014, LS-0022, LS-0026, LS-0035 in the subject area "Sunday School Leadership" in the Christian Growth Study Plan.

A Place for Everyone: A Guide for Special Education Bible Teaching-Reaching Ministry
Dewey Decimal Classification: 268.4
Subject Heading:
CHURCH WORK WITH THE HANDICAPPED\SPECIAL EDUCATION\MENTALLY HANDICAPPED—EDUCATION

Printed in the United States of America

Bible Teaching-Reaching Division
The Sunday School Board
of the Southern Baptist Convention
127 Ninth Avenue, North
Nashville, Tennessee 37234

*Permission is granted to make copies of information in the Appendix.

Table of Contents

Foreword

> **A Place for Everyone:**
> • **gives your church the tools to discover actions to take to make room for every type person and disability.**

Have you played musical chairs? It can be fun and quite entertaining, especially if there are a few type *A* personalities in the mix. It's fun until you are the one left out—standing with everyone else sitting. We must admit that we have all felt we cannot measure up and are excluded.

Billy was viewed that way. He was often excluded and left out. In fact, Billy never played musical chairs because he wore heavy braces on his legs and dragged them around on crutches. Billy and I grew up together—same school, same church. As children, we often treated Billy wrongly. We never included him in our games because he was different, odd, and out of place. But an amazing transformation took place as all of us matured. Billy was still Billy—disabled. But we saw him differently. He was always friendly, helpful, and joyful in the midst of his circumstances. We realized, fortunately and not too late, he didn't need us—we needed him. I don't know when it happened, but as we saw Billy for who he was on the inside and not for how he looked on the outside, Billy became a close friend to all of us. We benefited from being with him and knowing him. I remember the cheer, as if it were yesterday, when Billy pulled himself across the stage to receive his diploma.

Who are the Billys in your church? *A Place for Everyone* gives your church the tools to discover actions to take to make room for every type of Billy in your community. Isn't that what we are to be about? In Matthew 25, Jesus said, "As ye have done it unto one of the least of these . . . ye have done it unto me" (v. 40).

This book needs to be read by every pastor, staff member, and Sunday School director. It needs to be studied by everyone whom God has called to minister to those with special needs. Athalene McNay has given us an exhaustive practical work to help us begin or continue a vital ministry to people with special needs. My encouragement is, "Don't stop the music, continue the game, and this time, add another chair!"

Steve Cretin
Director
Ministry and Leadership Development Department
Bible Teaching-Reaching Division

A Place for Unconditional Loving

A place for unconditional loving:
- ministers to all persons.
- affirms the worth of persons with disabilities.
- helps persons with disabilities have the opportunity to know God's love through Jesus.
- provides acceptance and participation for persons who are disabled.

Many parents have made the statement, "If I could just find one Sunday School, no matter the denomination, that would accept my child with special needs, I'd go there." Is there really a place in the church for those persons with special needs?

The Concept of Love

In order to lay a foundation for ministry to persons who have special needs, we must go to God's Word, the Bible, and discover the mandate to minister to all persons. Regardless of their physical and/or mental disabilities, people need the Lord.

Love is the basis for ministry to all people and is the preeminent New Testament virtue. All Christians are mandated to express love through words and actions to all humanity. The writer of 1 John 4:19 stated, "We love, because He first loved us"(NASB),[1] which describes love as both God's action and our response. As a people who are loved unconditionally by God, we must we love unconditionally all people. Our response to the needs of people should never be lacking in love. The apostle Paul affirmed the necessity of love as we respond to the needs of people: "And if I give all my possessions to feed the poor . . . but do not have love, it profits me nothing"(1 Cor. 13:3, NASB). Deeds performed without love are shallow and lack meaning.

The needs of persons who are disabled provide an opportunity for the Christian community to respond in unconditional love. We are tempted, however, to be kind and compassionate toward some but not all. But when the Christian community recognizes the needs of all persons and responds effectively to their needs, then society as a whole will begin to perceive the relevancy of faith.

The love of a Christian for other persons exceeds humanitarian love. Helping others in the name of humanity is not sufficient, for God calls us to love and care for one another just as He loves and cares for us. Helping those who are weak and poor through Christmas baskets and governmental programs are only expressions of humanitarian love and concern. Christian love demands the ultimate gift of oneself.

The church shows love when she willingly complies with the accessibility guidelines of the Americans with Disabilities Act (ADA); when she provides sign language interpreters; when mentally retarded persons are included fully in worship and fellowship.

The church is mandated by the Scriptures and by the examples set forth by Christ to minister to the needs of all people. How shall we respond?

---

[1]From the *New American Standard Bible*. © The Lockman Foundation, 1960, 1962, 1963, 1968, 1971, 1972, 1973, 1975, 1977. Used by permission. Subsequent quotations are marked NASB.

The introduction was written by C. Von Reynolds, pastor, First Baptist Church, Seneca, South Carolina.

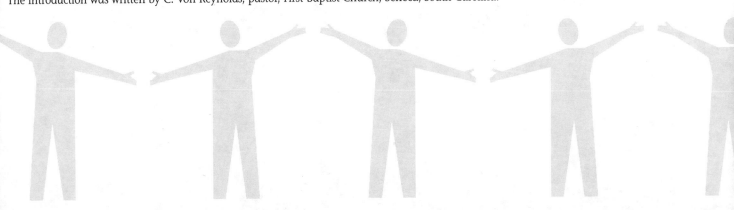

A Place for Reaching

A place for reaching:
- **reaches with a purpose.**
- **makes and initiates contacts.**
- **moves into the community and into homes.**
- **searches out nontraditional areas for caring such as in group homes.**

"That boy won't hurt you."

I remember that Dad paused a few seconds before responding to my comments. I remember an evening worship service, a small church building in early summer with open windows, and insects flying toward the ceiling lights. I remember the scent of Dad's aftershave and the strength in his powerful body as I leaned against him. As a seven-year-old I had never seen a person with cerebral palsy before. I remember the young man's short-sleeved shirt and the friend or brother who sat next to him. I remember the young man's twisted facial features and jerky movements. He smiled at me. I remember my fear and curiosity. I remember trying to tell Dad about it as we walked home after church. I remember Dad's sensitivity to my unspoken question. I remember that his acceptance of that young man's presence at worship laid a foundation of acceptance in me.

This chapter is about discovering and enlisting people to study the Bible. It is about welcoming the people we know and meet to our Bible studies and times of worship. That means we do not assume they want to come, or that they know we want them to come. It means expending effort and energy to invite people to our churches. It involves making plans to meet specific goals.

Persons with disabilities are like you and me. As a matter of fact, when it comes down to it, they are you and me. But often, persons with disabilities are called *exceptional people* because they are the exception to the way the majority acts, thinks, and learns. These people often need special education interventions or special adaptive aids to help them learn, get around, or communicate. The range of persons is wide with an even wider range of needs.

Are you a pastor or a deacon? Do you teach a Sunday School class or sing in the choir? Are you the minister of education or the Sunday School director? Do you direct a Baptist association or a state Baptist convention? Are you a staff person or state Baptist convention worker who happens to have a disability? When was the first time you encountered a person with physical or mental disabilities? Did you discover and enlist such a person to study the Bible at your church? How?

The purpose of this book is to remind us the church needs to be a place for everyone, regardless of their needs, and many exceptional people and their families living in our communities are waiting for us to reach out and involve them in our churches.

The logo on the cover of this book emphasizes the importance of including all persons in the life and work of the local church. All of us, including those with special needs, combine to create the mosaic of a church family.

Reaching with a Purpose

Forty-nine million Americans have disabilities. It is estimated that 10 to 20 percent of a community's population will include exceptional people. Many states provide for six-to-eight different types of special needs in their public school districts. These special needs may include those who are:
- mentally handicapped.
- physically disabled.
- visually impaired or blind.
- learning disabled.
- hearing impaired or deaf.
- multidisabled.
- behavior disordered.
- exceptionally bright.

For any one person with disabilities, there are 2 to 4 family members who are affected by the disability. Many of these millions are unsaved and unchurched. Over 90 percent of all churches do not have any type of purposeful ministry in any of the areas of special education

This "Letter to the Editor" was written by an angry mother.

"Children with mental handicaps are not welcomed in churches. Children's programs are for everyone, but not for the child who cannot think and do things like children her own age. Children's programs in most churches are well-planned for children who can perform at their age level or better, but they are not for the child with mental handicaps. My child and I cannot be a part of your church. Churches do not want my child with mental handicaps."

Whether a church could minister to that child in traditional ways or would need to develop a ministry unique to that situation, the mother's cry for acceptance for her child and herself echoes throughout every state. This mother expressed her frustration publicly. Many families do not.

I met a friend who told me about his profoundly mentally handicapped son who lives in an institution in another state.

"You're the first person in this state I've ever told about him. My wife and I decided to keep

Areas of Special Education

Mental retardation is a condition which causes a person's intellectual and social development to be much lower than most other persons of the same age. Three levels of mental retardation are:

mild	moderate	severe/profound

A *visual impairment* is a condition which causes a person's vision to be 20/200 or worse, even with the aid of corrective lenses.

A person with a *learning disability* has *normal or higher intelligence* but has problems in understanding language which may result in low levels of ability in:

listening	thinking	talking	reading
writing	spelling	math	memory

Gifted refers to significantly above-average intelligence or talents that require special attention to nurture and develop.

A *physical disability* is a *permanent* condition which hinders a person's ability to carry out the activities of daily living by a limitation of movement.

A *multiple handicap* is any combination of two or more disabilities.

Other areas of special education:
- deaf/hearing impairments
- speech impairments
- traumatic brain injury
- behavior disorders
- autism

our heartache to ourselves."

His colleague spoke with me later. "You know, most people don't know that our son is a paraplegic. He's grown, and the accident happened after he was married. We decided not to burden others with our problems."

Persons with special needs, or their family members, are found in every strata, every age group of the church. From departments for the youngest of babies to the most senior of adults, each has someone who is touched by disabilities.

Reaching out means we have tools in place to minister to their needs. Reaching out means we meet people who, in turn, minister to us.

> Our friend David is a math whiz with an aptitude for mechanics. He is also deaf. His talents are well-used as he teaches other deaf people the Bible.
>
> Ramon's legs were cut off at his knees in the line of duty. He is not a patrol officer any more, but he still does an excellent job leading a men's Bible study.
>
> Mrs. Carmichael spent her last years confined to bed. She spent her days praying for each member of our church.
>
> Eric is so bright! His insights challenge us; yet his questions cause us to look beyond pat answers and explore the depths and riches of the Bible
>
> MaryAnn told me that the years spent as Nora's advocate have been more rewarding for her than for Nora. "I may have been there to help Nora make decisions about where to live and how to manage her money, but she has taught me more about the things in life that really count!"

Reaching out means following the example of Jesus Christ who ministered to people with disabilities and showed us God's love and pronouncement of worth is for all persons.

Making Contacts

Do you feel impressed to develop a ministry for persons with disabilities? Does your church currently support some type of ministry? How do you contact the people who would benefit from this ministry?

Start by being truly aware of the people around you every day. Remember the three simple words we had to repeat as children? *Stop, Look,* and *Listen* before you cross the street. Those three words hold powerful implications in other things we do such as relating to people. *Stop, Look, and Listen* to the needs of people around you.

- Get acquainted with the coworker who is the parent (often a single-again parent) of a disabled child.
- Listen to the woman who checks your groceries at your favorite market as she tells you about her husband who had a stroke.
- Attend a parent-support-group meeting. Those parents are anxious to tell you about their children.
- Survey your church members to discover people who should be reached through such a ministry.
- Develop friendships with exceptional people and engage in everyday things that both of you can do such as going out to eat or to see a movie, talking, or taking part in sporting events.
- Be a volunteer in your local school programs. Learn about the services your community provides to persons with disabilities. Become informed about the

different exceptionalities. Get to know children's names.
- Volunteer at local and state events. Contact your local chapter of the Arc (formerly the Association for Retarded Citizens). Be a host at Special Olympics events. Offer to let a support group use your church building once a month; provide refreshments and childcare services free-of-charge.
- Talk. Start a word-of-mouth campaign. Ask your friends to introduce you to their friends who have disabilities. Get names, addresses, and phone numbers so you can call or write people directly. Tell them your church has or is beginning a ministry for people with disabilities and ask if they would like to be part of it.

Reach into the Community

Advertise. Let others know what you are doing. Be visible.

Develop a brochure about the ministry. Distribute the brochure at stores and at your public library.

Make certain the ministry is listed on every type of publicity piece your church uses: brochures, Yellow Pages™ ads, or bulletins. Decorate a bulletin board in a well-used concourse in your church building.

Be an active member of one of the support groups you have encountered.

Host an Information Day in your church fellowship hall. Invite all agencies and churches who provide services and ministry to disabled persons in your community. Ask each agency and church to set up a booth to provide information about the services they provide.

Reach into Homes

More than most groups, exceptional people and their families need to see your sincerity. A visit into their home or an invitation to your home is the most powerful contact you can make. These people are delighted to share about themselves and their daily routines. Parents of children who are disabled especially encourage you to see how they work with their child at home and to ask questions about how you can transfer that knowledge to your class. Plan and prepare your visits. Call ahead to make an appointment. Adjust your schedule to fit the family's schedule.

Arrive on time.

Always take a class member or another teacher with you.

Have a purpose for going. Take a church brochure or worship bulletin to prospects. Take the latest copy of *The Sunday School Leader*[1] magazine, *Special Education Today*[1] magazine, or other helps for the parent or caregiver.

Keep the visit brief. Be genuine and friendly. Don't be afraid to ask questions that will help you be a better teacher.

Visit in the home of each regular attender at least twice each year. Make note of any information about the member or her family to share with other church workers or church members.

If the prospect is a child or an adult with a mental handicap, take a self-developing picture of her and the other teacher (or a class member). Give the picture to the child to keep in her room as a reminder of your visit. Or give her a picture of the group of teachers in your department. This will help her "know" the teachers before she comes to Sunday School. Play an audiocassette recording of a greeting and invitation from class members. Show a photo album of members and their activities.

One teacher of youth likes "pop-in parties." After making proper arrangements, he and two class members take soft drinks and snacks and "pop in" to a prospect's home for an impromptu get-together.

Record each visit you make.

Reach into Group Homes

Many adults with mental handicaps don't live in traditional home settings. Throughout the country the familiar group home where 10 to 15 adults live in a congregate setting is being replaced with down-sized living arrangements.

You may find that adults in your area of the country are living in a house of 3-to-8 persons plus live-in house staff. It is important that you know the types of adult residential centers that operate in your area and that you are known to the people who work in those centers or oversee the program.

The house staff often changes each week. Meet each set of house managers so that they know you and your interest.

Know the name and interests of each person living in the same home with your class member.

Invite the entire group home to class parties and special events

Volunteer to help with at least one group-home activity each year. Act as a sponsor or provide refreshments.

Sponsor a fun night one Friday each month. Invite all the group homes in your area. Meet at the church. Ask house managers to provide transportation to and from the church. Some house managers may be required to stay with the group because of certain medical conditions. Otherwise, invite them to enjoy a "managers night out" for two hours. Play games, provide snacks, and sing songs; tell the Bible story from the next Sunday's lesson; and do an activity to reinforce biblical truths.

Conduct a session of Vacation Bible School one night each week for five weeks.

Offer to take individuals shopping each week.

Form a network of people who would each be willing to invite group-home residents to their houses for a holiday. Many persons living in group homes do not have a place to go, especially on Christmas. Be sensitive to residents who do not receive birthday or Christmas presents.

Know that agencies across the country are helping people live in apartments without the aid of full-time staff. Do not forget to include these persons in your group home ministry.

A *place for reaching* means a place to plan and provide for persons with disabilities because:
• God loves them.
• Jesus ministered to them.
• millions of people need to be part of the church.
• all other ministries can benefit.
• persons with special needs minister to you.
• the rewards are positive.
• such ministry is evangelistic.

---

[1]Order these materials from Customer Service Service, 127 Ninth Avenue, North, Nashville, Tennessee 37234-0113; FAX (615) 251-5933; or e-mail to CompuServe ID 70423,2526.

Q&A

Do you know anyone like this? Place check marks by the ones that apply.
___ a young child who wears leg braces
___ a parent of a physically or mentally handicapped child
___ a highly intelligent, but troubled, teen
___ an adult who has suffered a stroke
___ a group-home resident
___ a person who is deaf

Write the names of two persons you know who have disabilities but do not go to church. Pray for them now. Thank God for their lives. Ask Him to show you how you can enlist them in Bible study.

1. _____   2. _____

Look in your area telephone directory for names of support organizations, schools, or work centers for persons with disabilities. List here three of the names and telephone numbers.

1. _____

2. _____

3. _____

Give seven reasons why your church should reach out to persons with disabilities.

1. _____

2. _____

3. _____

4. _____

5. _____

6. _____

7. _____

A MOTHER'S PRAYER

The following prayer is dedicated to teachers who have helped my son and others like him. May this be the prayer of all who are dedicated to God's work.

Dear Lord,

I lift up my child, who has a disability, to You for Your love and care. I praise Your name for the mighty works seen through prayer already answered.

Teach me to forgive and love, as You forgive and love me, those who are jealous of our accomplishments and those who cannot endure our failures.

I pray that my child will be able to awake each morning with anticipation of the purposeful pursuit of the day. I pray for a quality life with activities, work, school, or play appropriate to his chronological age; for an independent life suited to his special needs; for a life with dignity, accomplishment, and acceptance.

Please open the eyes of people called by Your name, because they will be the instruments by which you answer this prayer.

Amen

A Place for Teaching

A place for teaching:
- creates a positive learning environment.
- adapts activities.
- provides age-appropriate activities.
- follows a session schedule.
- uses a variety of teaching methods.

"I liked hearing that God loves me. I never knew that before."

Don was 68 years old when he said those words to me. He had been attending our Sunday School class for several months. Like the other members of the class, Don was an adult with mental handicaps. His life story was a classic tale of abuse, abandonment, and exploitation. Don had never attended church until one of our class members invited him to Sunday School because we were having a dinner and fellowship after the worship service. When we had an evangelistic lesson four months later, Don asked us to tell him how to know Jesus in a personal way. He then asked for baptism and church membership. Don's eyes and demeanor reflected joy and peace after his profession of faith in Jesus Christ. I learned he died last summer at the age of 74. Praise God for Don's salvation! Thank God for a class where we could tell him about God's love for all people!

The focus of this chapter is on teaching, in the Sunday School setting, biblical principles and truths to adults with mental handicaps. The chapter assumes that there will be a separate, self-contained class for these adults. Most of what is discussed also transfers to teaching these adults through other learning opportunities.

For those who have been teaching an adult special education class for many years, this discussion is intended to encourage you in the way you are teaching. Or perhaps you can gain new ideas and fresh insights that will make learning enjoyable and spontaneous for both you and your class members.

If you are a new teacher in a special education Sunday School, you may wonder, *How do I teach these people? What do I do?*

This chapter tries to answer these questions by discussing the value of a positive learning environment and some teaching methods that have been effective with adults with mental handicaps. It offers you the benefit of collective knowledge from some people who minister in this area.

The Separate Department

By the time persons with mental disabilities reach adulthood, the gap between their intellectual and social skills/development and those of their age-group peers has become so great they probably will not learn as much in a regular class. A separate department works best for older youth and adults. Some adults with mental disabilities are married. Those couples may want to attend their regular age-group department, and in those cases every effort should be made to help them do so successfully.

Some young adults whose handicaps are less involved may want to attend the mainstream class with their age peers. This will work if other class members are sensitive and supportive. All attempts should be made by the Person/Family-Centered Plan (See example in Appendix.) to include higher functioning young adults and older youth in the social and recreational activities of their age group.

Susan grew up in the church where I was a member. She attended regular Sunday School classes until we formed one for adults with mental handicaps. Because she had mild mental retardation, Susan joined our class. She drove her own car, held good community-based jobs, handled her own money. I asked her if she were comfortable in our class and reminded her that she had the choice of attending a class with other young adults. I knew the department would welcome her. She declined, saying she knew she was different from those adults. She learned more in our class.

Ernie, on the other hand, did not grow up in that church. He also had mild mental retardation and visual disabilities. He tried to attend the regular class for young adults but did not have the social skills that helped him be accepted into that group. Some of his behaviors were disruptive and inappropriate for his age. The same department that would accept Susan was not sensitive to Ernie and did not want him there.

A Positive Learning Environment

Persons with mental handicaps respond best to a structured (but not a rigid) learning environment. Part of that structure not only follows a consistent teaching schedule that provides a secure routine but also allows for flexibility.

Maintaining a good teacher-member ratio is part of developing a positive learning environment.Whenever possible, try to follow these ideal ratios:

Characteristics of Persons Who Have Mental Retardation

Mental retardation is a condition which causes a person's intellectual and social development to be much lower than most other persons of the same age.

Persons who have mild mental retardation:
• have no distinctive physical appearance.
• are marginally independent.
• are often described as "slow."
• have difficulty with paying attention, verbal communication, memory skills, motivation, and social development.

Persons who have moderate mental retardation:
• have difficulty dealing with abstract ideas, transferring what they have learned to a new situation, and communicating.
• are emotionally immature and have an underdeveloped self-concept.
• are most likely to achieve success in the areas of self-help skills and social skills.
• require supervision.
• may have physical traits which cause them to appear "different."

Persons who have severe or profound mental retardation:
• are likely to have additional handicapping conditions.
• may be unable to communicate with intelligible speech, to walk, or to care for their personal needs.
• fail to respond to physical or visual prompting, but they tend to respond more rapidly when taught one-on-one.
• develop quite slowly.
• are dependent and require constant supervision.

- 1:1 for severely disabled members, ceiling enrollment of 6 per group;
- 1:4 for higher ability members, 15 members per group;
- 1:2 or 1:3 for persons with skills in between, ceiling enrollment of 12 per group

A minimum of two teachers is always needed, preferably one male and one female.

All teachers should know what to do in case of medical emergencies. Get first-aid training through your local Red Cross or ask your area group homes where their house managers get training. Before you begin, check with your church staff about any limitations on the church insurance policy. Be certain you know the medical alerts and concerns of all members. If your members come from an ICFMR (Intermediate Care for Mentally Retarded Adults) facility or if a medically-fragile member lives at home, plan to have a nonteaching assistant, familiar with specific medical needs, to be in the room at all times.

A positive learning environment happens when the teacher knows the learning strengths and weaknesses of the learners. Persons who have mental disabilities learn in the same ways as nondisabled persons. The significant difference is the speed or pace of learning. Generally, there is a qualitative difference in the way the person with mental disabilities sees the relationship between concepts and the degree to which she can handle abstract concepts. She needs concepts expressed in simple or concrete terms.

There are no unique teaching methods for teaching persons with mental disabilities. Teachers do need to be flexible and able to adapt standard teaching methods to facilitate the learning experience.

Adapting Activities

Some activities will need to be adapted for the members to be able to grasp the concept being taught. Following are some points to keep in mind when adapting activities.

1. Know the learners well. Know how each member learns and the skills he or she can exercise successfully without frustration.
2. Think of the adaptation as an adjustment to fit members' needs.
3. Use common sense.
4. Allow learners to do everything they can for themselves.
5. Slow the pace.
6. Express concepts in simple terms. Provide real-life examples and concrete experiences. Give only one concept at a time.
7. Plan for extra individual attention.

When introducing new activities or concepts, keep in mind the following guidelines.
- Be brief.
- Present each step in sequence. Be aware that you may need to back up and present the step again.
- Make success possible at each step.
- Repeat. Repeat. Repeat.
- Present the concept in a variety of ways.
- Make applications to situations your members will know.
- Reduce visual and auditory distractions.
- Introduce new vocabulary words before telling new stories.
- Provide an outline of important points.
- Use pictures and other visual aids with all activities.
- Use materials that are of high interest and low level of difficulty.

Low Level Readers or Nonreaders

Many adults with mental handicaps read on a low level, or they are nonreaders. Adapt for them in the following ways.

- Use pictures.
- Record instructions on an audiocassette.
- Use diagrams and line drawings.
- Use color coding, shape coding, number coding, or texture coding.
- Place a pattern over important words to help with word-search and crossword puzzles.
- Use role play, music, movement activities.

Nonverbal Members

Some members are not able to communicate verbally. Use the following suggestions to work with those members who have difficulty communicating.

- Use the communication system that works for each member: gestures, sign language, a picture board or book, an electronic communication device.
- Ask questions that can be answered by nodding or shaking the head. Or use signs mounted on dowel rods—green circle for *yes*, red circle for *no*.
- Provide nonverbal ways the member can participate in singing (play a rhythm instrument) and drama (pantomime parts).
- Use visual activities and pictures that require the member to point, follow broken lines, or match symbols.
- Remember that 70 percent of all communication is nonverbal. Use the skills you already have to understand the nonverbal member and talk to him as though he can respond verbally.

Learning Activities

The old saying, "Involve me, and I will understand," is especially true for the person with mental disabilities. Like most of us, he will remember more if he learns by discovery. Learning activities are those direct, purposeful experiences which allow him opportunities to retain what he hears and sees.

Learning activities should be used in each part of the teaching session. Examples and types of learning activities that can be adapted for use in any session are found in this chapter. The key to using these activities rests on what you know about the unique mix of your members' skills and abilities. Not all members can do the same activity in the same way. Consider each member's skills levels, group members according to their skills, and plan activities for that group.

Activities should meet these criteria:

Be age-appropriate.—Is it an activity that a member of the regular age-group class would do? Adults with mental disabilities do not want to be treated like small children. Wilda and her husband came to the evening Vacation Bible School held for adults in their small town. They knew their limitations, but they were proud of their jobs and marriage. The VBS teacher asked each person in their group to make handprints on white paper. Wilda started to cry. She was frustrated. "I'm 35 years old. I don't want to do baby work."

Relate.—Does the activity relate to the emphasis and biblical truth for that session? Every song, picture, and game must be a tool you use to help members focus on what you are teaching. Adam's teacher wanted him to know that God gives us good food to eat. Because Adam is nonverbal, his teacher asked Adam to point to simple pictures of fruits and vegetables, and she planned a game about making good food choices. When they had a healthy snack, the teacher thanked God for good food to eat and led Adam to nod for his Amen.

Be relevant.—Biblical truths must be relevant to what is going on in members' lives today. If lives are changed and affected and if you help members apply Bible truth to their everyday living, then what you teach must have meaning for the things that are happening now.

Jenny wanted her class to remember God is with us when we are afraid. Jenny asked a member to name a time when he is afraid. Jenny then led that member to thank God for being with him at that time.

When planning activities, remember:

* the purpose of the activity and how it relates to the purpose of the session.
* your space and resources.
* the time—do you need to enrich, shorten, or do preliminary steps? Will the activity frustrate or bore members?
* to provide a variety of activities in each session.

A Session

A typical Sunday School session is 45-60 minutes long. One schedule suggestion that works well:

* **The Hook**—Capturing members' interest. (5-10 min.).—This time is called "Create Learning Readiness" in *Special Education Teacher Packet*.[1] It involves planning activities that help members prepare to learn about the session emphasis. These activities are usually conducted in small groups.

* **The Book** and **The Look**—Hearing the Bible story, singing songs, learning a Bible verse is the emphasis during this time. (20-25 min.)—This time is called "Guide Bible Study" in the *Special Education Teacher Packet*. This involves the core of the study, using the Bible as the textbook for the class. Members meet in one large group for this time.

The church offers adults with mental handicaps opportunities to know God and His Word. Bible truths meet real needs and change people's lives. Especially in Sunday School, all activities should help members discover all-important biblical truths.

Because telling the Bible story is the major activity in Sunday School, teachers should prepare for teaching all week long.

1. Begin studying the Bible passage early in the week.
2. Have a personal daily quiet time.
3. Write a brief central truth about the Bible passage that class members need to know. This is "Bible Truth" in *Special Education Teacher Packet*.
4. Read the Bible story in the curriculum resource such as *Special Education Bible Study*[1] member's book.
5. Circle and change words that are too hard for your members to understand.
6. Underline the points you wish to stress.

Many people think telling the Bible story is merely that—telling the story by the lecture method. Basically, lecture is the foundation for telling a story, but there are many ways to vary and adapt a lecture which will keep members attentive and interested. Make a lecture more productive by using:

* varied voice inflection
* understandable vocabulary
* visual aids
* familiar illustrations
* good eye contact with the listener

Movement of a Lesson

God's Word	Our World	
Past	Present	Future

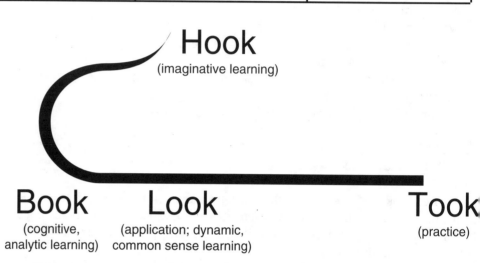

Hook
(imaginative learning)

Book
(cognitive,
analytic learning)

Look
(application; dynamic,
common sense learning)

Took
(practice)

- good time limits
- well-developed questions
- appropriate activities

Use all of these each time you tell the Bible story to persons with mental disabilities. Even the one with profound mental disability who does not seem to comprehend what you are saying can benefit.

Involve members in a variety of ways as you tell the Bible story. Make it the most enjoyable learning activity of the session.

Open Bibles.—Provide an easy-to-read Bible (third- to sixth-grade reading level) for each member in the department. Direct members to open their Bibles to the Scripture passage each session. Nonreaders want to be included in this; mark their Bibles before the session begins.

Present the basic facts.—Show a teaching picture. Tell the story briefly the first time. For this example, 1 Samuel 3:1-10 is used. Say: *Today we will hear about Samuel. He lived with Eli the priest. One night Samuel heard Someone call his name. Samuel thought it was Eli, but Samuel learned that God was calling his name.*

Go into more detail.—This is where the teacher can choose to tell the story, ask another church member to portray the key character (Samuel tells the story in first person), involve members in a drama (provide biblical costumes or hand-manipulated figures and a script). This tells the story a second time.

Keep it short.—Do not tell everything you know. The Bible story should not be more than three to five minutes. Before the session begins, know what you are going to say and stay with your selected points. Even members with higher abilities cannot handle great theological discussions.

Review the facts.—Adapt at least one activity to review the highlights of the story. Ask: *Did Samuel live with Eli the priest? Was Samuel alone in his room one night? Did Samuel hear Someone call his name? Did Samuel say, "Speak, Lord, for Your servant is listening"*(1 Sam. 3:9, NIV)?[2] Write questions that members can ask the man who portrays Samuel; ask volunteers to tell the story using the teaching picture. This tells the story a third time. Even with this much repetition, members may not have short-term recall about the story.

Make a transition statement.—Refer to the Bible story during the application activities. Say: *God had a message for Samuel. Samuel listened to what God said. God has a message for us today. We can listen to God's Word.*

Evaluate how you most often tell the Bible story:
- Is the vocabulary appropriate?
- How are members involved?
- Do I plan activities for each member's skill level?
- Are activities age-appropriate?
- Is the story presented more than one way?
- Is the story interesting?
- Are illustrations relevant to members' lives?
- Do I talk too much?
- Do I keep reasonable time limits?

- **The Took**—This involves applying biblical truths to situations in the member's life.(15-20 min.)—This time is called "Apply Bible Truth to Life" in *Special Education Teacher Packet*. This is the time when teachers help members realize how the Bible relates to their own lives.

- **The Closure**—Bring the session to a gradual halt.(5 min.)—This time is called "Close Session" in the *Special Education Teacher Packet*. It provides a time for a reverent finish and a transition time to the worship service or extended session.

Teaching Methods

Use Sign Language

Moving day. Our new house! We were busy unloading boxes. We already knew one of our new neighbor's boys, age six, was completely deaf. My husband looked across the lawn. Before I knew why, he was at the neighbor's front door.

"How do you sign 'watch for cars'?" he asked the mother.

She started signing, "Watch for."

She stopped abruptly. "Where is he?" she shouted.

My husband pointed to the street in front of the house. Scottie was racing his big-wheeled bike as fast as he could go, oblivious to anything around him. He wasn't watching for cars or his mother. She ran to the street and pulled Scottie and the bike into the driveway. As fast her fingers could fly, she said, "Young man. I've told you. Stay out of the street. Cars can kill you."

That was the beginning of our intrigue with sign language. By the way, Scottie's mother showed us other applied hand communication skills that day.

Our country has a fascination with sign language, and its popularity seems more evident each day. Signing, especially Signing Exact English (SEE), has made its way into many public school systems. Signing is also making its way into many churches both as SEE (more often used with children) and as American Sign

Language (ASL). ASL or Ameslan is reported to be the third most used language in the United States. Sign language is a visual-gesture language developed by deaf people to communicate with one another. It is a unique language where the learners use their eyes and hands to communicate.

What does this have to do with adults with mental handicaps? Sign language is not only for deaf people. In the expressive hand pictures of sign language, people learn to hear with their eyes and speak with their hands. It is logical and concrete and uses more than one learning modality. Many persons with mental disabilities who cannot speak otherwise are able to communicate with simple signs. Many persons with mental disabilities, who are verbal, love to sign because it is a most complete and expressive way to communicate.

Are you interested in learning sign language? People who sign want to teach you. Where can you find a sign language class and a teacher? Try contacting one of the options nearest you to learn sign language.

- Association for the Deaf and the Hard of Hearing
- Community college or university
- Public school continuing education classes or public school classes for the deaf
- Churches with ministries to deaf persons
- A parent of a deaf child
- Your state school for deaf children

It takes time to become a proficient signer, but even the person with a casual interest in signing can learn basic concepts and signs in a short time. A large number of well-illustrated learning guides show how to make signs and explain the concept or memory aid associated with each sign. Sign language is a versatile teaching tool, and the creative teacher can find many ways to use it.

Introduce vocabulary.—Work one-on-one with the severally disabled member. Point to people and objects either in the room or in a teaching picture. Demonstrate the sign slowly. Help the member practice signing as you point to the object and say the word.

In small groups of members with higher skills, create interest in the session. Practice the sign for an important word members will hear throughout the session. Or in large group, learn the signs for new words members will hear in the Bible story.

Sign the Bible verse.—Print a short Bible verse on poster board. Put an enlarged sign-language illustration under each word. Lead the nonreading member to "read" the verse with sign language.

Teach members the signs to a Bible verse as a tool to help them memorize the verse.

Ask members to sign a Bible verse with a partner to demonstrate one way we can share God's Word with other people.

Use signs on a rebus.—For the nonreader, substitute the pictures in a simple rebus with the illustrations of familiar signs.

Note that most songs and choruses repeat words and phrases to help emphasize the main concept in the song. Use illustrations of signs in place of the repeated words and phrases when making a song chart.

Sign songs.—All members, regardless of their reading skills, enjoy signing favorite songs. Help your members learn the signs to many of their favorite hymns. Learn new signs weekly. You will find a repetition of many signs throughout the hymns. This activity builds sign vocabulary quickly.

Lead members to write a praise to God using signs they know and a familiar tune. Direct them as they sign and sing their praises.

If your members are a part of a special education choir, make certain they sign one of their songs each time they perform for the church. At least once each year, arrange for your members to sign as the worship choir sings a special song arrangement. Invite other members of the congregation, including any who are deaf, to practice and perform with your members.

Prepare a long-playing videotape. Feature an interpreter signing as a soloist sings familiar hymns. Use these videos to plan an individual activity.

Sign prayer.—Encourage the nonverbal member to pray in sign language as you interpret. If she needs help praying, show her how to sign each word as you say a simple prayer.

Lead members to write a group prayer on a large sheet of paper.

Direct as the group reads and signs the prayer together.

Ask the deaf member to pray slowly in sign language as a hearing member or the entire group verbally interprets her prayer.

Ask volunteers in the large group to say: "I praise God because He is _____ _____." Ask each member to complete the thought in sign language.

Sign the Bible story.—Ask volunteers to tell, using sign language, what the Bible story was about.

Use low-vocabulary words to write a drama about the Bible story. Direct as volunteers speak their parts with sign language. Ask a member to read the verbal interpretation.

Arrange for an interpreter to sign the Bible story each session to the member who is deaf.

Use Music

"I can't sing. We don't have a piano in the room. None of us knows how to lead songs."

Excuses. I've heard several of them. Why don't teachers feel comfortable using music in their Sunday School departments? Are they self-conscious? Do teachers imagine they have to be highly-talented musicians? They don't, really. Persons with mental handicaps are the most accepting group I know. They don't mock or tease, or even hear if you sing off key. But they do enjoy singing and musical activities.

Music is the language of the soul. It stirs emotions and causes a response in all of us. People with disabilities respond to music in the same ways as do people without disabilities. And why not? We cannot respond incorrectly to music. There are no wrong answers or hard questions with it. Teachers who work with multidisabled children testify that music will reach them when other activities and stimuli do not. Music is always positive. Whether you like a certain type of music is a matter of personal taste. But music itself offers each of us a chance to grow and expand. Music offers adults with mental disabilities opportunities for self-expression and positive attitudes. It is a tool to help them remember, to communicate, to increase self-esteem.

As you think about the ways you use music with your members, keep these basic principles in mind.

1. Many nonmusical activities can involve music. Music can accompany the class on a walk around the room. It can provide a background as members plan a party. Teachers often sing instructions or praise members for appropriate behavior with simple tunes.

2. Music provides a way for each member to feel a part of the group. Even nonverbal or multidisabled members can move with the music, play a rhythm instrument, or take part in a game.

3. Music is an avenue for creative expression. Teachers use music to help nonverbal persons express moods. (Show me how you move when are sad, happy, tired, hungry.) Members who are frustrated or noncompliant can express their feelings by playing a musical instrument.

4. Music can be used to reinforce any learning activity and stimulate imagination. Members can sing a Bible verse, role-play a song, answer questions with musical sounds. They can even learn to listen for the music in

nature, such as singing birds, gentle breezes, falling rain.

5. Music is a gift from God to help us express our praises, know about the world and people around us, be aware of the bodies God created for us to use.

Music can be used to:

- motivate learning.
- reinforce learning.
- apply learning.
- express emotion.
- induce a quiet mood.
- regain self-control.
- encourage team work.
- build a sense of self-importance.
- strengthen social skills.

It is not important that the teacher sings well or knows fundamentals of music. It is important that the teacher use music each session; indeed, it is best when a teacher can use music more than one way each session.

Musical experiences can be rhythm, singing, using instruments, or body movement. The potential for using these in each part of the teaching session is unlimited.

A typical Sunday School session is 45-60 minutes long. One schedule suggestion using music that works well is:

Create Learning Readiness

- Lead members to clap a steady 1-2-3 rhythm. Play a recording of sounds relating to the Bible story. For example: modes of travel (the people of Israel travel to a new land), or sounds of nature (God made the world).
- Sing your welcome with a simple tune as members arrive; then use the same tune to sing an introduction to the Bible story. Invite members to sing with you each time.
- Lead members to play cymbals or tambourines as they prepare to learn about Bible-time worship.
- Play a cassette of African rhythm music as members take a nature walk.

Guide Bible Study

- Ask members to hum to the rhythm of the Bible verse.
- Call on volunteers to make up songs as they retell the Bible story.
- Direct nonverbal members to play shakers or small bells as others sing.
- Direct members to sway to the music as they sing the unit song.

Apply Bible Truth to Life

- Guide members to speak in rhythm, "Thank You, God. Thank You, God, for our homes and our jobs. Thank You, God."
- Ask volunteers to locate a song from the hymnal which relates to the main truth of the session.
- Lead members in a "wave" to express their willingness to obey God this week.
- Help a member play a tune on the Autoharp to express her response to God's call on her life this week.

Close Session

- Help members gain self-control with an ageless rhythm and hand movement: Roll them, roll them, roll them, roll them. Give a little clap. Roll them, roll them, roll them, roll

them. Lay them in your lap.
- Use a familiar tune as members sing and shake hands with each other: Shake a hand, shake a hand of a friend. Shake a hand. Please, don't be shy. Shake a hand, Shake a hand next to you. Now it's time to say good-bye.
- Play a recording of quiet music. Say, *This music reminds us to be quiet and respectful of others in the worship center.*

Who leads the singing in your department? What do you use for instrumental accompaniment?

Donna and Louise have led the music at our special education retreats many times. Louise has a great voice, and Donna plays any stringed instrument she can find. Louise is a children's teaching specialist for our county association of churches. These ladies only work with our members during special projects. Our adults enjoy Donna and Louise immensely because they bring a lively freshness to our group. Donna plays the guitar, the banjo, and the ukulele at these events. Louise teaches folk songs and fast-paced tunes in addition to the many wonderful Bible-related songs she knows. These women are so winsome. The nonverbal member and those hesitant to be part of the large group are soon drawn into the fun. Everyone is included. Donna invites all of them to play her instruments, including the members with low abilities. Donna and Louise know our members respond to music and try to use it in all the teaching situations.

Have you considered asking other church members to help with music? This is a bite-size responsibility that does not require the same preparation as teaching. It allows others opportunity to work in your department and still have time to be in their own classes. Having church members in the department unearths hidden talent and encourages people who never dreamed they could minister in Sunday School. It frees your time for other responsibilities in the department. If you are uncomfortable singing in front of groups, it solves your dilemma.

Have you thought about using different types of instrumental accompaniment? Even if you are fortunate enough to have a piano and pianist each week, you and your members will enjoy a variety of instruments to accompany your songs. Some examples are:

1. *Special Education Cassette Recording*[1] and tape player.
2. guitar and other stringed instruments.
3. electronic keyboard.
4. drums.
5. handbells.
6. cymbals.
7. tambourines.
8. wind instruments.
9. shakers.
10. hand chimes or soprano xylophone.

Ask your members or other people in your church or community. You may be surprised at the number of people who are willing to help one Sunday each month or for an entire month. Youth from middle school through high school have great technical skills. Remember to ask one of them.

Your members' disabilities may be so involved they do not tolerate loud and unusual noises. Use soft sounds on the electronic keyboard; sew small bells on the corners of washcloths; fill cylinder-shape containers with fine sand; play *Special Education Cassette Recording;* add other gentle-tone instruments. Be certain you introduce each instrument one at a time so members can adjust to them.

Use Prayer

We have already discussed ways we can use sign language and music with prayer. As a teaching tool, prayer helps us realize God is a person who loves us and is interested in our daily concerns, helps us learn to express our thoughts and feelings, and causes us to realize true strength and power exists outside of ourselves.

Teachers of persons with mental disabilities can use prayer in the one-on-one teaching time to help an individual regain control as a preparation to hear the Bible story; with the member who uses a communication board as a way to respond to biblical truths; to help members feel they are a part of the group; to teach about worship, praise, and thanksgiving.

Teachers can use prayer in ways other than listing prayer requests. Do you want to reinforce a Bible truth or Bible verse? Ask a member to thank God for it. Spontaneity is such a blessing. Do members share about the fun and exciting things that happened this week? Stop and thank God for them or learn to praise God.

Steve is paranoid and anxious much of the time, even when he's taking his medication. It's all a part of his mental illness. He enjoys Sunday School class because he feels secure and loved. One day Steve agreed to pray aloud, and I will never forget the tenderness in his voice. Steve didn't ask for anything; he just praised God: "Jesus, You are so sweet. God, You are kind. God never hurts me or makes fun of me. I love Him. Amen."

Who was the teacher at that moment?

Use Bible Verses

We often display a Bible verse for members to read and "learn" each week. The teaching procedures in the *Special Education Teaching Packet* offer a suggestion for an activity. We do an activity and then go on to something else. Possibly members can say the verse, but have they really learned something?

Remember to guide a discussion about the content of the verse each session. Ask questions about the verse. Explain what it means and ask members to repeat what you said. Call on members to tell what they think or feel as a result of hearing the verse. Refer to the verse during the application time. Help members transfer the verse's truths to what you are trying to teach them.

Whether you have a different verse each session or one each month, your members have the need to memorize Scripture. Your creative assistance can make the challenge easy and even fun. In addition to using sign language and music, you can illustrate each word with a symbol, shape, or picture. Use a low-vocabulary Bible translation for easier words to picture. Draw or cut pictures and symbols from outdated materials. Print the Bible verse on a card strip. Lead members to place the words in sequence. Illustrated verses benefit the member who is blind, especially if you use texture with the shape. He learns to identify the word with the shape. Guide him to put the shapes in sequence as he says the words.

Guide members to write a poem with the verse. Create or adapt a game to play with the verse. Print each word on matching color cards and play a game like Concentration™. Print the verse on a large poster and cover a different word each time you lead members to say the verse aloud.

Tape each member on an audio or videocassette as she says the verse alone. Lead her to say the verse along with her own voice when you play it for the group.

Use the Teacher

Whether you want to be or not, you, as the teacher, are the star attraction in Sunday School. Yes, you are trying to point members' attention to God. Yes, you want the focus to be on eternal truths. But the fact remains, you are a tangible and real presence. You represent all hat you teach to your members. Your teaching is more effective when you:

- mirror God's love and acceptance for each member.
- show enthusiasm and appreciation for God's Word.
- show the importance of Sunday School by well-prepared plans and by being in the room before the first member arrives.
- make certain your actions away from church are consistent with what you say at church.
- are open to listening to what each individual is trying to express.
- get involved in members' lives away from church.
- remember God uses the personality of those who serve Him. Learn your own teaching strengths and develop them.
- acknowledge your own teaching weaknesses. by taking advantage of every training opportunity and all available resources to turn those weaknesses into strengths.
- truly enjoy what you are doing.

Use Puzzles, Pictures, and the Arts

Puzzles.—Puzzles make fun and popular learning activities that are appropriate for people of all ages and skills levels. Puzzles involve multisensory stimuli, so they help us to learn and retain what we have learned.

Adults with mental handicaps like the challenges of puzzles, especially ones with built-in success. Most puzzles can be adapted to a member's level of functioning without embarrassing him. Puzzles can be used to teach a Bible verse, review a Bible story, or as an application activity.

Make a cut-apart puzzle for the low-skilled nonverbal member. Print a Bible verse, a yes-type question with the answer, or glue a picture to cardstock. Cut the cards into three large jigsaw shapes. If your members need a guide, position the puzzle on a larger sheet of cardstock and draw around each shape. Use this as a one-on-one activity. Cut-apart puzzles can also be cut with diagonal, straight, and angled lines.

Make a texture-coded puzzle for the visually impaired member. Print review statements on separate card strips, then cut each into two pieces. Glue matching textures of fabric or sandpaper to the back of each pair. As the member matches the pairs, read each part of the statement to her. Puzzles can be coded by number, sound, shape, and color.

Modify a word-search puzzle for nonreaders. Highlight the words in yellow and read each word as the member underlines it with another color. Or cover the puzzle with a pattern with the hidden words showing. Written puzzles can be coded puzzles, acrostics, crosswords, and fill-in-the-blanks.

You never need to wonder whether you use puzzles too often. Many members want to work some type each week. Well-adapted puzzles are a secure and comfortable activity for the member who is frustrated easily.

Pictures.—Pictures have always been the universal way to communicate. We learn to read the pictures in a book before we know the words. We use pictures with preschoolers, diagrams with upper grades, complicated formulas in advanced mathematics classes. People need visual aids.

In the Special Education Department, you will use three basic types of pictures:

1. biblical-teaching pictures relating to the content of the Bible stories.
2. real-life teaching pictures relating to a real-life story or situation.
3. activity pictures to help members review Bible facts, learn a Bible verse, apply a biblical truth.

You and your members can have the greatest fun using these in unlimited, creative ways.

- Feature pictures in a unit display.
- Direct members to imagine they are persons in the picture. Ask what they would feel or think in that situation. Or lead members in a picture pose.
- Make a chronology of a Bible hero's life.
- Build a creative writing assignment around a picture.
- Illustrate the meaning of a Bible verse.
- Create a gallery or unit wall of pictures to tie several sessions together.
- Make a pictorial song chart for the nonreader or a rebus so members can "read" parts of the story.
- Use simple pictures to introduce and build vocabulary or word recognition.
- Feature a "member of the month" and display pictures about her life. Or keep a department album of interesting class projects, fellowships, parties, and trips.
- Make games: sequence pictures, matching activities, or puzzles.
- Ask members to express what they feel or know by drawing pictures.

Special Education Bible Study and *Special Education Teacher Packet* provide all three basic-type pictures each session, both in the member book and on colorful teaching posters. You can find supplemental activity pictures in outdated materials, especially Adult Sunday School magazines. If you want to use larger biblical teaching pictures, ask children's workers if you can look through their picture files. Often, they will let you have duplicate copies. You can also order *Bible Discoverers Teaching Pictures, Bible Learners Teaching Pictures, or Bible Searchers Teaching Pictures*[1] which can be used along with special education materials. These picture packets also contain real-life pictures of children so a biblical picture may not be provided for every session. However, these teaching picture packets will allow you to build your own teaching picture file.

Remember to select pictures which contain age-appropriate content for adults. Be careful that real-life pictures do not show adults making poor or compromising choices. Choose pictures that are uncluttered and not visually "busy" so that members can easily tell what is happening in the picture.

Arts and crafts.—Arts and crafts are big items in many Special Education Sunday School classes. The value and appropriateness for using them is often debated.

The pro side says:
- members love to draw and color.
- craft activities hold interest and hold down behavior problems.
- members use the projects to decorate their rooms at home.
- members are accustomed to using craft projects.
- crafts are good time-fillers.

The con side says:
- members should learn other activities.
- other adults don't do crafts in Sunday School.
- crafts may be viewed as busy work by the learner negating their ability to teach biblical truths.
- other well-planned activities can hold interest and control behavior problems.
- the members' Sunday School magazine is a more appropriate take-home item.

Who is right? What about using arts and crafts in Sunday School?

The primary task of Sunday School is to teach the Bible. All curriculum should be centered around that goal. The next task is to make choices that will respect the adultness of members, that will not open them to ridicule. We want to help members learn in ways acceptable to adults.

We want to help adults with mental handicaps realize biblical truths are for their everyday ives. Do arts and crafts keep us from those goals? For the mere sake of doing them, arts and crafts are not a valuable curriculum choice. As a teaching tool or a relevant project, arts and crafts can be a well-developed curriculum choice.

Many experienced teachers say their members, representing a wide range of skill abilities, do not want to do craft projects in Sunday School. These adults attend work activity centers and community-based jobs and are accustomed to doing what other adults do. They seem to be selective, agreeing to some art activities but balking at others.

Corella has taught a special education Sunday School class for 30 years. She is a loving and compassionate teacher who knows her members and spends time with them away from church. Many of the members have been in the class from its beginning, starting when they were children and youth. Most of them are nonreaders and nonverbal. Some still live at home with upper-age parents and do not attend a work program of any kind. Corella says her members expect a coloring activity when they arrive each Sunday. In fact, the class schedule has not changed much over the years. They sing the same songs and tell the Bible story in much the same way. Corella finds this is less disturbing to her members and helps them feel secure.

Jim doesn't do crafts in Sunday School. He thinks it will make his adults with mental handicaps look childish and open them to ridicule.

Jim likes to do the craft projects at special education retreat. Jim is exceptionally good at woodworking and enjoys the challenge of modifying wood projects the participants can use at home. He says that while members work with him, he can catch many teachable moments to relate biblical truths to their lives.

If your teaching style falls somewhere between that of Corella and Jim, and most do, you approach arts and crafts on a once-in-a-while basis. At times, teaching procedures suggest a craft or art activity or the teacher knows an activity that will help her members understand truth. But crafts are not used every Sunday. Instead, special education teachers choose to use arts and crafts in VBS, for missions projects, at Christmastime for a party, for an activity to illustrate a biblical truth or a relevant application in extended sessions, during scheduled arts/crafts/game nights, or in the design of displays and bulletin boards.

If you do use art and craft activities, keep these tips in mind.
1. Use felt-tip markers or colored pencils rather than crayons.
2. Use glue sticks instead of glue.
3. Use modeling clay rather than play dough.
4. Use colored chalk and water color pencils and other supplies you might find in an art store.
5. Plan projects that can be completed in one session.
6. If preparations require the use of power tools, do these before the session begins.
7. Always allow members a choice of activities and do not expect that every member will want to participate in the project.
8. Have puff paints, fabric paints, glitter, and other texture mediums for the visually impaired member. When possible, include her in three-dimensional projects.

Use Drama

This is one type of activity that can be used every session. If you doubt there is a bit of a "ham" in each of us, you need to attend one of our special education retreats. I have seen people who have never spoken and who exhibit all types of delayed social responses take small roles and put their hearts and souls into their parts. It is wonderful and exciting.

Betty came with her upper-age mother that weekend. Betty was 38 years old, and this was the first time she had attended anything social with other adults like herself. She didn't say much because she was not sure of herself. While her mother attended the parent sessions, Betty mostly watched her group's activities. Then we acted out a Bible event and asked Betty to say three small words, "There he is." We practiced the parts and actions, and the more we practiced, the more Betty got into her part. By the time we did the skit for the parents, Betty was a pro. She did her piece and stopped to look at her mother with eyes shining. Her mother was surprised and proud, but not as proud as Betty was.

Drama helps us identify with other people and their feelings. Drama helps us put on the mask of another personality and exhibit a boldness we can't display at other times. Drama is a mulitsensory activity and can help us learn more quickly and retain information longer. Drama is often a team effort. It helps us learn to work in a group and to appreciate each member's contribution. Drama can be used in each part of the teaching session and can be combined with other teaching methods such as art, music, sign language, or creative writing. Drama preparation can require time to write a script, or it can be impromptu. Drama can be a narrative, a group reading, spoken parts, or a pantomime. Members enjoy them all. You can use drama:

- as a role play to create learning readiness.
- when a guest tells the Bible story from a first-person perspective.
- to review the Bible story through a picture pose or acting out the Bible story.
- as members apply Bible truths by acting out real-life situations they have written.

Jack, a 43-year-old man with mental disabilities, could not read many words, and this embarrassed him. The first time we asked him to take part in a drama activity he was hesitant. Finally, he whispered his fear to me, "They'll find out I can't read." I explained he did not need to know how to read, and that most of "them" could not read either. We practiced a choral reading. Jack had one short line to memorize, which he said perfectly. He held his paper as if he were reading. Jack did a great job, and his face glowed with pride. His teachers said Jack talked about that skit for 12 months. The next year at our retreat, Jack was the first to ask if we were going to do another skit.

When using drama, be certain to follow these general guidelines:

- Assign roles based on the member's skills abilities.
- Plan for readers, nonreaders, and nonverbal members.
- Don't expect perfection. Guide each member through her part of the drama step-by-step.
- Allow for members' input and creativity.
- Expect them to ad-lib and to be impromptu.
- Practice, even if the "performance" is brief and that same day.
- Don't limit the size of the cast. You can have one actor if you have a class of one. Or you can have two or three groups performing the small skit if you have a large department. In that case, try to vary the type of skit. For instance, one group can pantomime Samuel hearing God's call; the next group can do a choral reading; another can do an interview with Samuel and Eli about the call. Include teachers in the drama when possible.

What is the key word for providing a positive learning environment for adults with mental disabilities? Abilities. As a teacher to emphasize what each member is able to do; what you are able to do to help that person learn better; and what God is able to do in that person's life because of your willingness to know and teach him or her. Give praise generously.

---

[1]Order these materials from Customer Service Service, 127 Ninth Avenue, North, Nashville, Tennessee 37234-0113; FAX (615) 251-5933; or e-mail to CompuServe ID 70423,2526.
[2]From the Holy Bible, *New International Version*, copyright © 1973, 1978, 1984 by International Bible Society. Subsequent quotations are marked NIV.

Q&A

Write a brief description of your current Sunday School schedule. How does it compare to the schedule suggested in this chapter?

_____

_____

_____

_____

Describe how you can use each of these teaching tools in your present Sunday School class or department.

• drama _____

• sign language _____

• music _____

Write a poem about 1 Samuel 3:10b: "Speak for your servant is listening" (NIV). Choose a familiar tune and sing the words of your poem.

_____

_____

_____

_____

Describe two things you discovered in this chapter.

_____

_____

_____

A Place for Mainstreaming

> A place for mainstreaming:
> • defines what mainstreaming is.
> • knows when mainstreaming is best.
> • provides a general know-how of teaching helps.
> • addresses common problems and solutions with mainstreaming.
> • provides for an accessible church building.

Jason's parents were members of the church before they married. Jason's birth was eagerly anticipated by the other church members because at that church any new baby is "our baby." He was welcomed with open arms. When it was discovered Jason was born with cerebral palsy, the preschool teachers provided appropriate learning opportunities for him in each age-group class until he was ready to promote to a first-grade class. There will be a place for Jason in the regular children's program for as long as he attends that church. Even with his limited verbal skills and physical disabilities, Jason is included.

Patricia has been a minister of education, minister to children, a writer of Children's

Sunday School curriculum. She knows and loves children. When it came time for Jason to move from the Preschool Division to the Children's Division, there was no question in her mind that he would be in a regular class. She worked with Jason's parents and the Sunday School teachers to ensure a proper place for Jason.

This chapter is about inclusion. It is about opening doors to all persons who want to be part of God's church. It is a plea against excluding any person from your church because of his or her disability.

No matter where you serve or teach in your church, no matter how long you have been at the job, this chapter is for you. Awareness of special needs is to each part of the church program what reading is to each part of a school curriculum; there is no part, no division that can do without it. Just as we use reading in all types of study, we need to use a knowledge base about the needs of exceptional persons in all types of ministry.

This chapter is about a role the church played at one time in history, and then forgot how to play. It is about remembering our priorities and returning to a time when worth of the individual in our churches depended on the individual being one of us, a child of God.

What Does Mainstreaming Mean?

Mainstreaming is placing eligible exceptional persons in the same class with their age-group peers for instructional and social reasons. It also means a place in all church programs and ministries for eligible exceptional persons to benefit and serve along with their peers.

What is the mainstream of your church? Sunday School, worship services, Discipleship Training, visitation, VBS? Others? There are exceptional persons who want to be included in those ministries.

Mainstreaming is for which exceptional persons? Look again at the list of disabilities in Chapter 1. Mainstreaming is for most of them. Notice the term *eligible exceptional persons*. Later in this chapter, we will discuss the times when it is best not to mainstream. For now, we can be sure that the majority of exceptional persons need to be in the church mainstream.

What is inclusion, and what is exclusion? What does it mean to welcome and make someone part of something? What does it mean to shut people out and keep them from being part of the group? Exceptional people fear the rejection and embarrassment of being unwanted and ignored in church. They want to be welcomed to activities other than just the Sunday morning worship service. Mainstreaming means looking at our history.

Christians make it a point to come together in worship and praise. Psalm 145:3 says, "Great is the Lord and most worthy of praise" (NIV).[1] Church is a fellowship of people who know the love and forgiveness of God. It is the only organization whose Founder stressed restoration and complete acceptance.

Jesus included all people in His earthly ministry. He does not exclude. He accepts all who have been rejected. He makes everyone equal.

The church is a partnership of all people who trust Jesus Christ as Savior. It is a partnership of diverse backgrounds which come together to learn, grow, encourage, and labor together for the gospel.

No matter where you live or the current size of your local fellowship, somewhere in the beginnings of your church is a nucleus of people who came together for worship. That nucleus worked together, prayed together, and determined to grow bigger. They developed a closeness, a bonding, a common vision. Everyone was a welcomed addition. Then came the growth.

A fellowship of believers began work less than 60 years ago. In the fledgling years, each person was a welcomed contributor. If a person had a disability, so what? The disability was a part of him or her, in some cases, a minor drawback that needed to be worked around. The important thing was the person who had joined the ranks. Church growth and expansion of the work came rapidly, and with it a concern about the church's image. Church members wanted star achievers in their ranks, people they could brag about. They didn't want those in high, visible positions who were too smart, too twisted, or too impaired. The church wanted to woo and win prospects with its sharp, average-American image. The church didn't want others to think it was a fellowship of losers. The focus was shifted from inclusion to exclusion. They went from acceptance to discrimination. What about your church?

Mainstreaming means we look back to where we started to see if we got off course. Mainstreaming means looking at our purpose.

That purpose was given to us by Jesus. He entrusted His followers with a responsibility like no other. He gave us the keys to heaven and a charge to invite all who would to come and dine.

If I were to ask each of you, "What is the function of the church?" I would most likely hear:
• to tell other people about God's love.
• to share the good news and lead others to a saving faith in Jesus Christ.
• to meet with other believers in a corporate time of worship, praise, and study.
All of those answers would be true.

What if I were to ask: Which people? Which believers? Would the answer be the lame, the blind, the deaf, the intellectually superior? Or do we modify our purpose in subtle, qualitative ways?

Mainstreaming means we honestly evaluate how we formulate and strategize our purpose. Mainstreaming means looking at restrictions. What limits our outreach? What gets in the way of making our churches places for everyone?

Do the values of society govern our churches? Is the worth of an individual performance-based? Do we know how limited our perspectives are compared to God's? Do we remember we can see only a tiny portion of the total picture? Do we weigh potential and usefulness in terms of our own standards? Have we forgotten how much each person falls short of the potential God planned for us at creation? Do we admit we have prejudices? We all do. Do we ask God for the power to overcome them? Do we understand how threatened we are by anything that reminds us of our own frailties and failures? Do we know sometimes we are afraid a disability will "rub off on us" and contaminate us?

Mainstreaming Means Looking at Our Opportunities

The Americans with Disabilities Act (ADA) was signed into law on July 26, 1990, with the purpose of providing a national mandate to protect persons with disabilities from discrimination and other social injustices. For Christians, the ADA is an example of people getting around to doing what God told them to do a long time ago.

The church is in a prime position to model the spirit of the ADA. As an organization, the church can be a social leader for justice, acceptance, and compassion.

- The church starts with a pastor who understands the viable outreach potential in identifying persons with disabilities in his community.
- The church continues with a study in the Scripture of the way Jesus modeled compassion when He ministered on earth.
- The church goes on as church members evaluate, for persons with special needs, the accessibility of church programs and the church facility.
- The church encourages persons with disabilities to come to church, and the church needs to have a sensitivity to the unique needs of their families.

Mainstreaming becomes a reality when the church helps persons with disabilities live as independently as possible, employ an eligible disabled person, and encourage persons with disabilities to use their talents and gifts in the church.

Why Mainstream?

Mainstreaming provides the church with increased outreach into the community. Mainstreaming in the church is a tangible way to live what we teach. A church that openly cares about the needs of all people gains the respect of the people around it.

Mainstreaming capitalizes on the manpower churches have available in their limited number of volunteers. Often mainstreaming creates a place to serve, a manageable area of responsibility for the member who doesn't think he or she has time or talent for "bigger" jobs.

Mainstreaming allows teachers and other workers to increase their ability to serve God in their field of ministry. Mainstreaming is best:

- in the Preschool Division with the infant who has been diagnosed with physical disabilities.—Preschool is where young children learn early to socialize with people different from themselves. So mainstreaming gives the average child opportunity to learn acceptance early in life. Preschool teachers know and use teaching strategies that help both the nondisabled and the disabled young body develop, young mind to be aware, and young soul to know and appreciate the love of God.
- in the Children's Division with the child who has mental disabilities.—Her chronological interests and social needs are in line with those of her age-group peers. Mainstreaming is effective as the member works on an adapted activity with her peers at the small-group table, in combination with one-on-one help.
- in the Youth Division with the teen who has struggled with learning disabilities all his life.—This hidden disability attacks and wears at self-esteem. Academic failures and frustration in our competitive society, coupled with the insecurities of the teen-age years, create turmoil and social problems. Mainstreaming is where the youth worker reaches out and loves a hurting youth.
- in the young adult department with the intellectually superior young father who exhibits leadership skills.—Mainstreaming provides opportunity for him to exercise his creativity and develop his skills for use in God's service.
- in the middle-age adult department with the woman who has become blind.—Mainstreaming provides the social contacts and emotional support that she needs from her fellow Sunday School members.
- in the senior adult department with those whose bodies have gotten old.—Mainstreaming causes the church to evaluate the church building and to provide ramps and conveniently placed restrooms in the senior adult area.

• in the singles department with the single-again mother of a multidisabled child.— Mainstreaming opens opportunities to meet practical needs in nontraditional and creative ways.

Mainstreaming is not best:
• when the gap between skills development and those of age-group peers widens with adults and some youth with mental handicaps.
• when persons have multiple disabilities.
• when the structure of the curriculum is not appropriate for the type of disability.
• when disabilities are so involved or severe that individuals require constant one-on-one attention.
• when disruptive behaviors are totally inappropriate for the age level.
• when the person's level of comprehension is far below that of age-group peers.
• when a physical disability is so involved that the person cannot attend church.
• when an individual is so medically fragile that life-threatening seizures or upper-respiratory arrest are always a strong possibility.

In situations when mainstreaming is not best, a separate department may meet the needs of persons who are disabled.

What Is Integration?

Integration allows for the exceptional person in a separate department to spend a portion of the Sunday School time with her nondisabled peers. Examples of successful integration strategies are:
• adults who are deaf meet with their age-group peers for fellowship and announcements before the actual teaching begins.
• children with mental disabilities join their age-group peers for recreation during VBS.
• youth with autism attend the first 15 minutes of the worship service each Sunday.

Integration methods have been used in many churches for several years. The methods are a deliberate attempt to ensure that the exceptional person is not completely isolated from the rest of the church family. Integration is a way that makes the church a "less restrictive environment." Teachers involved in integration strategies give the following tips.
• All teachers, helpers, and department directors must work together and have clear goals for what they want integration to accomplish.
• Before beginning, introduce the idea of integration to all members who will participate and get their input into the planning.
• Plan definite times for integration opportunities and interaction. Don't just "let things happen."
• Encourage church staff and other visible leaders to model acceptance and interaction with exceptional persons.
• Children with disabilities need to be able to share classrooms, play space, and small-group time with their nondisabled peers.
• Offer praise when integration takes place. For instance: One teacher displays, on a bulletin board in a main concourse at her church, photographs of children in appropriate integration play. One youth leader presents award certificates to youth who help serve the annual special education banquet at their church. The presentation takes place before the entire congregation at the beginning of a worship service.

Common Problems with Mainstreaming

Some problems exist with mainstreaming, such as:
- expectations on both the part of parents and workers who have unrealistic ideas about what the child can do.
- a lack of knowledge about disabilities and the church's role in meeting special needs.
- uncertainty on the part of teachers about how to teach exceptional persons and fear that extra work may be involved.
- a negative attitude about disabilities in general or about specific inappropriate behaviors.

Solutions for Mainstreaming

Make resource materials, such as *Special Education Today*,[2] magazine available to parents and teachers.

For preschoolers and children, consult an early intervention specialist and schoolteachers who are familiar with the child. Develop church goals that are supportive and consistent with school goals.

Commend Sunday School teachers for using teaching methods and skills they already know. Provide "how-to" materials that help teachers adapt their materials for the exceptional member.

Invite the pastor and other church leaders to activities and events for persons with disabilities.

It is easier to mainstream and integrate younger children. All preschoolers with disabilities should be placed in their age-group class. As gaps widen between their skills and those of their peers, teachers may need to consider retaining a prekindergarten child while his or her peers move ahead. In most cases, a preschooler in church should not be kept more than two years behind his age peers. There are exceptions when the degree of disability involvement is severe. In those cases, preschool workers should support parents as they make choices about early childhood intervention centers. Preschool teachers need to continue to integrate the disabled child as much as possible with nondisabled preschoolers.

Mainstreaming is usually the best choice for all children. All children's curriculum series offer suggestions for adapting materials and integration for every age group. It is much easier to find volunteers who will commit to work one-on-one with an exceptional child in the mainstream class than to find teachers for a separate class. Many such volunteers have said they want to work in Sunday School, but they cannot take on the preparation of full-time teaching. The opportunity to serve as a helper in the class of a special-needs child is a customized solution to this problem.

Take turns working one-on-one with the exceptional child who is mainstreamed in your class. Give all teachers a chance to know her and give her a chance to know all teachers.

Younger youth and some older youth with mental disabilities are successful in the mainstream program. Mainstreaming is appropriate if the disabled youth has higher skills and is socially accepted by nondisabled youth. Some clues may be taken by watching the interaction of the youth.

1. Is the disabled youth included in small-group conversations or ignored?
2. Do other youth initiate interaction with him, or is he always trying to enter into their conversations?
3. Do nondisabled youth accept the disabled youth in their fellowship?

If older youth are separated, every attempt should be made to include them in the social and recreational events of the youth department. Teachers need to teach socially acceptable behaviors, and teachers need to teach that integration is based on acceptance and understanding.

The only adults who should be in a separate class are those with mental disabilities. The other exception may be a class for persons who are deaf. This is considered a language ministry.

Deaf adults remind us that they are persons with a unique culture. Even though hearing impairments are part of special education programs in public schools, deaf adults realize their exceptionality has to do with the language they use. For that reason, most deaf adults prefer to learn in a separate department that uses their language. Because of the increased popularity of sign language and because hearing children have been taught not to be afraid of the differences between themselves and deaf persons, some younger deaf adults are seeking friendships among young hearing adults. Occasionally, these deaf persons attend a mainstream class with an interpreter. Either way, the social needs of deaf adults in church should not be ignored. Churches need to encourage other adults to learn simple signs and ways to communicate so deaf adults can take part in other mainstream events.

Adapting Curriculum Materials

Exceptional persons learn in the same ways as other people although their learning pace may vary significantly. There are no unique teaching methods. Successful teaching comes from knowing the student and her learning strengths and weaknesses and the way she likes to learn. It is important to know which skills she has and which skills she finds difficult and frustrating. It is also important to know how you need to adapt or adjust the teaching activities to make the learning environment comfortable and positive.

Adaptation is simply a matter of adjusting to a different situation or condition. As a wise and articulate writer put it, "If there is a traffic jam on the way to work, you take another route." That is most descriptive of what the teacher must do with planned teaching activities. If the exceptional person in your class runs into a road block with your standard teaching activities, you can quickly take another route.

In general, all people learn through the three senses.

Hearing and Speaking (auditory/linguistic learner)—The Word Player

Seeing (visual/spatial learner)—The Visualizer

Touching and Moving (tactile/kinesthetic learner)—The Mover

Learning styles vary with each person, but most people exhibit a strength in one of these three ways as a preferred learning style.

The *word player* learns best when he repeats what he hears. This learner learns best in a quiet room with books or tape recordings of information. He likes to read and to write and learns best when he can listen to information, write it down, and listen to it again. He follows oral and written directions well.

The *visualizer* learns best when he can see things in his mind. He may be a doodler and daydreamer; he may like to look at the pictures, maps, or diagrams; he may draw, design, and create.

The *mover* learns best when she can move. She likes games and activities and likes to touch and feel what she is looking at. The mover would rather be active than sit and listen to a lecture.

Learners ask four general types of questions:

The *imaginative learner* asks, Why do I need to know this?

The *analytic learner* asks, What do I need to know?

The *common sense learner* asks, How does it work?

The *dynamic learner* asks, What can this become?

In addition, learners can be social (interpersonal) or individual (intrapersonal). A wise teacher knows that each individual may be a unique combination of learning styles and questions, and the teacher needs to present information through more than one of the senses. The more a teacher can use different senses, the more the member will learn.

Learners also learn more when they are involved. Some educators have called this the discovery or inquiry method. Instead of merely listening to a lecture, learners gain more if they answer questions, do problem solving and application, have a choice about what they learn, use their imaginations, express their feelings, or act on their motivation for learning.

Experienced teachers like to stress that all students bring extra baggage with them to any learning environment such as:

• home background.

• socioeconomic background.

• cultural values.

• fears and prejudices.

• self-esteem and personality.

Exceptional persons often bring additional baggage to church such as:

• rejections.

• failures.

• positive and negative church experiences.

• a need to feel worth and hope.

• challenging questions.

• untapped talents.

• unique outlooks on life.

So what does all this information about learning styles have to do with the exceptional person in the church mainstream? It serves to remind the teacher that exceptional people are more like than unlike their age-group peers.

Any challenges of adapting curriculum material to meet the needs of exceptional persons can be minimized as the teacher understands persons with disabilities are persons trying to meet the pressures of life and to make the most of their abilities in spite of their disabilities.

Read the suggestions given on the next pages. Perhaps they will help you feel confident about teaching exceptional persons mainstreamed in age-group classes.

Persons with Visual Impairments

A person is legally blind if he sees at 20 feet what a normal-sighted person sees at 200 (20/200 vision). Physical sight may be impaired in these forms—vision may be blurred, or vision may be restricted totally or in part.

One person may not be able to tell darkness from light, while another can make that distinction but not be able to differentiate shapes. Central vision (detail and color) may be destroyed totally or in part; peripheral vision may be reduced. Color vision may be defective, especially when differentiating between red and green. The ability to adapt from dark to light or light back to dark may be slow. Extreme sensitivity to light may be experienced.

Persons with visual impairments are not born with any more hearing ability than sighted persons. Sensory abilities come from cultivation and practice. Motor development may proceed slowly, due in part to the absence of visual lures. Blind people may fear falling or getting hurt. Social development may demand more effort because often communication is nonverbal. Only 10 percent of all individuals labeled as blind encounter total darkness all of the time.

Visually handicapped, visually impaired, visually limited, and *blind* refer to persons whose impairment is severe enough to hinder learning.

Adaptations

Some adaptations may be necessary when working with persons with visual impairment.

Lighting.—Avoid harsh lighting. Don't seat the member facing the glare of a window. Find out if additional sunlight in the room helps. Find out if you need to shine a desk light on close-up work.

Room.—Keep the room uncluttered and items off the floor. Have a nonskid walking surface. Don't use throw rugs. Help the member learn the location of items in the room; then keep the room consistent. If you need to move things, inform the member. Cover sharp corners of furniture. Place bright strips on stair edges.

Equipment.—Provide large-print reading materials including Bibles and hymnals, Braille materials (when appropriate), tape cassettes and recorders. You may also need to have magnifying devices, electronic communication devices such as Braille computer, opticon,™ tellatouch,™ and large tables to hold these pieces of equipment.

Class participation.—Use each of the senses, especially touch and auditory. Don't forget the sight sense. Smile and use the same facial expressions you use with normal-sighted persons.

Use a combination of activities that require large and small amounts of eye work. Use brightly colored pictures and visuals with simple patterns. Avoid clutter and stripes. Encourage the member to sit as close as possible to visuals. When using visuals, verbalize what you write and see. Give directions and procedures in simple, clear steps. Make certain the member knows the class schedule and inform her about changes in advance.

When working with a child who is visually impaired or limited, simplify complicated activities and vocabulary. When using printed materials, ask a sighted friend to read. Remember that word recognition can be delayed in a totally blind child or one with severe impairments. Be ready to explain any new words the member may hear in your class.

Use more audio aids than visual aids when teaching a class of adults who have severe visual impairments or who are totally blind. Use discussion and question/answer teaching methods.

Offer assistance for finding a chair, giving written responses, and learning the layout of a room or the building. Let the totally blind person hold your arm at the bended elbow when walking.

Remember that persons with visual disabilities do not want preferential treatment, instead they want you to be considerate of their condition. Look at the person when you talk and speak in a normal tone. Use words that refer to sight such as *look* and *see*.

If you teach a person who is blind and deaf, be quick to identify yourself when you approach her. Never leave her sitting alone in an unfamiliar place. When walking with her, keep her informed of upcoming doorways, stairs, vehicles, and changes in terrain and slopes. Use the communication devices she knows best. Many blind-deaf persons are often adept at pulling in information from their other senses, and they read American Sign Language by placing their hands lightly on the hands of the signer.

Minister to People Who Are Visually Disabled

Several opportunities exist to minister to people who are visually disabled.

- Sponsor fellowships and support groups.
- Provide housecleaning assistance and transportation.
- Act as as reader and friend to blind students in a nearby college.
- Transfer printed materials to audiocassette tapes or Braille.
- Take them out to dinner or have them come to your home.

Encourage visually disabled persons to minister in your church:

- as Sunday School teachers.
- as prayer partners.
- as instrumental or vocal musicians.
- as a pastor.
- as leaders.

Meet Francis. She has been totally blind since she was a baby. By the time I met her, Francis had retired from a civil service career. She shares her two-bedroom house with her guide dog. Friends and family drive her to church, the store, and her many social activities. Her life is so organized! I've never seen kitchen cabinets and closets like hers, with everything marked and grouped systematically. She has one luxury—weekly maid service. "I don't like dust on the furniture. I can smell it," she says.

Persons with Learning Disabilities

As high as 10 percent of the population have some type of learning disability. Learning disabilities are caused by a dysfunction in the way the person's brain processes visual and audio information.

If you teach a regular age-group class in your church, you probably have at least one member who has a learning disability.

Professionals do not agree on one precise definition of learning disabilities. They have tried to establish one for years, but there are as many specific characteristics as there are people who have learning disabilities. Although it is difficult to simplify these characteristics into one typical profile, professionals do agree that persons with learning disabilities:

- have normal or higher intelligence.
- do not achieve academically at the same level as their peers.
- exhibit low levels of achievement in one or all: listening, thinking, memory.
- have difficulties with one or all: writing, reading, and math.
- do not have the disability due to emotional overlays, visual or hearing disabilities, or mental handicaps.

Professionals also agree that persons with learning disabilities exhibit the common characteristics of:

- low self-esteem.
- low motivation.
- poor concentration.
- difficulty in making appropriate social judgments.

Learning disabilities are often described as hidden handicaps. The person may not be aware he has a specific disability. He only knows the sense of failure he has

encountered many times in school and other learning opportunities. He often thinks he is dumb, is sensitive to criticism (real or imagined), is self-critical, feels he has nothing to contribute to his group or society. That is where the role of the church becomes so important in the life of a person with learning disabilities.

The child is eager to find praise and encouragement. The teen yearns for affirmation and sense of worth. He needs help determining goals that will keep him out of trouble. The adult would like a learning opportunity where she will not be embarrassed or humiliated, where he talents are noticed and appreciated.

Maybe you've known a person like Willie John. In Vacation Bible School he was the constant energy dynamo. Church workers didn't know about learning disabilities then. They knew little boys his age can be active and fidgety. His speech was not as mature as the speech of some of the rest of the children, but he was only five years old. Teachers would give in, cajole, then get harsh with him, all in the same three hours. It was the same at Sunday School, extended service, and Discipleship Training. Willie John's parents came to everything and brought him.

By the time Willie John reached the Children's Division, he looked for ways to disturb the boys' class with his jokes and horseplay. He didn't like to read aloud. It was too difficult for him, and the other boys laughed when he made mistakes.

In his teen years, Willie John balked at going to church. When he came, he slouched in hi chair at the back of the large-group area with his arms folded and his head down. He listened to the discussions, and occasionally he had something to say. But church was not a pleasant place for him. Neither was school.

Willie John stopped going to church when he got married. He never did overcome the reading difficulty, and he was afraid someone would ask him to read or, worse yet, be a teacher. But after his children were born, he went occasionally with his wife to church service. Soon he noticed the church could use his knowledge in sound systems and electronics, and Willie John has served his church in that capacity for many years. No one but his wife knows why he hesitates to be in Sunday School and other small-group classes.

The church holds a choice position to improve the self-esteem of a person with a learning disability as we:

display respect for him.—Never embarrass or label him a troublemaker.

help her know and develop her talents and skills.— Find one thing she can do well and encourage her to stretch in many directions.

support his parents.—Help them understand their own feelings of self-worth may affect those of their child.

give positive, focused attention.—Praise, your time, and boasting about her accomplishments are priceless gifts.

set clearly defined rules.—Rules for behavior and consequences for inappropriate behavior help children realize a sense of responsibility for their own behaviors.

establish her belonging to the group.—Responsibility in class or other organized activities reaffirms she is a member of the church family.

actively allow the youth with learning disabilities to express his feelings.—Have informal discussion groups that identify problems and concerns he may have. Role-play situations and develop problem-solving strategies.

Adaptations

Provide a structured, well-organized learning environment. Make certain the member knows schedules and time limits. Be consistent. Limit choices of activities and keep time limits short but flexible.

Keep directions simple and clear. Try to use one-step directions when possible. Ask the member to repeat directions to you in his own words to check for understanding. Print multistep directions on a large sheet of paper. It helps to tape record directions so the member can replay them.

Tell the member what to listen for before you tell the Bible story.

Provide an area free from distraction for the person who has a problem with concentration.

Keep lectures short. Review Bible stories with an activity that allows the member to move. Keep verbal instructions and commands short, no longer than 10 seconds.

Allow the fidgety child to change seats, take a short break, or sit closer to a friend. This can help the child to keep focused on the lesson.

Develop creative ways to repeat and drill information frequently. Relate all new information to prior knowledge.

Know the member's learning strengths and make certain she has an opportunity to use those in your class. If your member is a youth with learning disabilities, ask her what is hard and what is easy for her to do.

Be generous with praise and positive feedback. Help the member feel safe and not threatened in the learning environment. If you must talk to him about his behavior, do it privately.

Use as many senses as possible. Use drama, music, art, and videos in place of pencil/paper tasks. Use visuals and cues to aid attention and memory. Adapt activities that require writing to one-word answers.

Encourage the member to sit close to a buddy or near the teacher and in the front of the room. Provide opportunities for her to work on small-group projects where she can contribute to the team effort.

Start with a concrete concept and move to the abstract. Break assignments into small steps. Shorten long activities by asking the member to do only the ones circled or every other one.

Adapt reading activities by rewriting materials using words the member knows. Be careful not to make this too simple since that can discourage him. Assign a reading buddy to read the material orally. Allow the member with learning disabilities to read softly to herself instead of silently. Allow time for the member to highlight words she doesn't know in a Bible verse and to learn them before she reads or says the verse aloud. Restate the main ideas of the reading material in simpler terms before he starts to read. Encourage him to use a bookmark or other familiar technique as a line marker or to help him track as he reads.

You may not know if a member in your class has a learning disability. Even when parents of children and teens are aware of the disability, they may hesitate to tell the teacher at church for fear the child will be labeled as dumb. You can develop your awareness of the person who may have a learning disability by observing some common clues. But be careful you do not try to diagnose learning disabilities from these clues. Instead, use them to develop sensitivity about the teaching strategies you may need to use.

1. Is the child shy?
2. Is he or she disinterested or unaware of what is taking place?
3. Does he ask irrelevant questions or give irrelevant answers?
4. Is she easily distracted by external stimuli?
5. Does he fail to interact appropriately with his peers? Does he exhibit disruptive behavior? Does he overreact to stimuli?
6. Does she appear to be confused or frustrated?
7. Does he read and understand at a level lower than his peers?
8. Does she have trouble with oral and written directions?

If you work with older preschoolers (ages four and five), be sensitive to excessive

behavior problems, problems with meaningful social interactions, extreme delays in language developments. Be careful how you approach any parent of a child you may suspect has a learning disability or possibly another disability. Since your observations alone are not enough to make an accurate diagnosis, try offering workshops on early childhood learning disorders. These can help parents get the information they need to seek professional help. If you think you should speak to parents, talk first with others who know the child and his history.

Sal's behavior problems and lack of self-control were getting out of hand by the time he was four years old. Church workers were ready to approach his mother about the possibility of Attention Deficit Hyperactivity Disorder (ADHD) or learning disabilities. A wise worker in Mom's Day Out asked Willa, the preschool director, to observe Sal for a few weeks. Willa watched how Sal did close-up work, watched videos, and played on recreational equipment. It became apparent to her that Sal had a problem with his eyes. She wondered if a visual problem could cause him to be so hyper. Before talking to his mother (by now quite sensitive about her child's behavior), Willa talked with the grandmother who agreed to approach the parents about taking Sal to an ophthalmologist specializing in children. In a few weeks, Sal was wearing strong corrective lenses. His behavior changed drastically.

Persons with Attention Deficit Hyperactivity Disorder

ADHD is not a new problem. Persons with this disorder have been labeled many ways, including disobedient, hyper, brain-damaged. But, although it is not new, it is an issue that causes parents and teachers much concern these days.

Controversy about ADHD exists among three main groups.

Some education professionals do not recognize ADHD as a disability or a health disorder, thereby limiting the types of services the student can receive in school. Educators say the diagnosis of ADHD is based on behavior scales that are nothing more than subjective judgments. Educators express concern that the production of Ritalin, the medication most commonly used as treatment, has increased almost 500 percent in the past five to six years. The argument is made that the only disorder is the one that exists between a child and a specific environment, that a diagnosis of ADHD is a convenient excuse for uncontrolled behavior. The question is asked, Do parents excuse the child's wrong behavior with a diagnosis of ADHD?

A large number of parents are concerned with the epidemic-size numbers of their children who are labeled ADHD. Estimates are that 3 to 20 percent of the population have ADHD. These parents are asking, Do schools excuse negative behavior with a diagnosis that removes any responsibility from the child?

Another group of parents is asking: Where are the answers? Do you know what it is like to live with an ADHD child? Do you think we don't try to make our child behave? Do you think we want to excuse his poor performance by saying he is merely inattentive?

What Is ADHD?

ADHD has been described in a number of ways. Some of them are as follows.
  • It is a neurodevelopmental disorder (by doctors).

- It is a behavior disorder (by psychologists).
- It is a chemical or metabolic disorder (by nutritionists).

ADHD is a pattern of hyperactive-impulsive behavior and/or severe and persistent inattention behavior that exhibits itself early in the individual's life.

ADHD is *not* a learning disability. However, certain other conditions occur frequently with ADHD:

- learning disabilities, especially with written language.
- communication disorders.
- anxiety.
- Tourette's syndrome.
- mood disorders such as depression and bipolar disorder.
- disruptive behaviors such as oppositional disorders and conduct disorders.

ADHD diagnosis is based on these observable behaviors:

- lacks sustained attention.
- makes careless mistakes.
- does not listen when spoken to directly.
- cannot follow instructions.
- does not organize tasks.
- dislikes and avoids tasks requiring sustained mental attention.
- loses work materials.
- is distracted easily.
- forgets daily activities.
- is hyperactive-impulsive.
- fidgets or squirms in seat.
- displays restless, excessive, inappropriate movement.
- cannot remain seated
- cannot wait his turn.
- does not take part in leisure activities quietly.
- acts as if "driven by a motor."
- talks excessively.
- blurts out answers before questions have been completed.
- interrupts or intrudes on others.

In addition, the symptoms must have occurred since early childhood, have occurred for at least six months, are present in two or more settings (i.e. home, school, and church), and must indicate a significant impairment in the child's social relationships and academic functioning. Because all children display these behaviors at some time, diagnosis of ADHD must be made by professionals in conjunction with other diagnostic tools and procedures.

Children with ADHD

Children with ADHD:

- cannot seem to screen out things that distract them from their task.
- cannot seem to keep their bodies from moving all the time.
- display quick changes and extremes in emotions—from happy to frustrated to anger to forgetting in a short amount of time
- appear not to think before they act or speak; they are aggressive and often destructive.
- have difficulty conforming to rules.—Unless there are clear and immediate

consequences, their impetuous behaviors will get them into trouble for the same offense again and again. This behavior pattern is one of the primary problems ADHD children face. They do not seem to learn from discipline measures, and adults see their behavior as willful disobedience.

- have difficulty responding to reward systems.—ADHD children display a strong need for immediate gratification. Effective rewards must be given frequently over short amounts of time. However, ADHD children are less likely to work for a reward and more likely to work harder to avoid negative consequences.

Working with an ADHD Child

- Display clearly written rules with specific consequences. Be consistent and provide consequences immediately.
- Give immediate, consistent, and tangible rewards for appropriate behavior. Give him twice as many positive statements as negative.
- Let her know you love and accept her even when you reject her behavior.
- Use private visual reminders to get his attention and help him stay on task.
- assign a positive role-model buddy.
- Try to remain calm even when the child's behavior is disruptive.
- Stand close to her and provide a verbal reprimand without sarcasm. Never ridicule her in front of other children.
- Maintain open communication with the home. Provide support and information for his parents.
- Work as a team with other church workers and the parents to create a structured and supportive environment.
- Provide evidence of faith in action. Make certain the child with ADHD can see God is real and active in your life. Give the child tangible evidence God loves all of us in spite of our sins and failures.

Working with the ADHD Teen

- Help him identify his strengths and encourage him to use them.
- Find ways to go with her and other teachers each month on a special outing.
- Maintain good communication with him. Listen when he talks.
- Provide structure, but allow her to have some ownership in decisions that affect her.
- Provide positive feedback, meaningful rewards and consequences.
- Provide a learning environment with short breaks and opportunities for active responses.
- Remember the parents.

Jamie is an older teen with ADHD. His behavior problems were evident when he was 18 months old. At home and church, he aggressively hurt other children and destroyed property. His parents tried many ways to manage his behavior from rewards, to talking, to spankings. Nothing helped. Even his own siblings did not want to be around him much. By the time he reached high school, Jamie had a history of problems with teachers, academic failures, and rejections. Although he was, and still is, gifted and creative, Jamie was able to finish high school only in an alternative setting. Church is no longer for him. The members of the youth group made him the brunt of too many comments and jokes. Jamie does not believe Christians can show love and understanding since he seldom received that from them.

Coping with ADHD

ADHD is currently one of the most researched childhood conditions. Professionals do not agree on its cause, except to say that it is a physical disability of some sort. Professionals do agree a "missing link" strongly affects the behavior of the person. Parents of children with ADHD are often desperate to find that missing link. One mother said: "I will leave no stone unturned even though my son's behavior offers me no hope. My hurts over my son's condition have left me exhausted, but I will not give up the fight to help him have a normal, productive life."

The controversy surrounding ADHD points to many children, treated with medication for ADHD, whose behavior problems are not observable away from school. Agreeably, these may be children who just do not like the learning environment or who are merely exhibiting bratty behavior. It is not the responsibility of the church to make a judgment in that controversy.

Professionals remind us that though persons with ADHD do not look disabled, they are handicapped when it comes to fitting in with society. The role of the church is to mirror God's love and support.

Remind parents of these general principles.

1. Try to understand why your child behaves as he does.
2. Make certain your expectations are appropriate for his age.
3. Punish aggressive and harmful behavior.
4. Focus on expected behavior instead of what he does that is wrong. For example say, "Put all four legs of the chair on the floor" rather than "Don't lean back in your chair."
5. Encourage your child to do her best.
6. Provide as much structure and consistency as possible among home, school, and church.

If you know an adult with ADHD, learn what you can about ADHD. You can obtain information from books and professional magazines relating to ADHD. Ask your local school district or write:

CH.A.D.D.
499 N.W. 70th Avenue, Suite 308
Plantation, FL 33317
or
National Coaching Network
P.O.Box 353
LaFayette Hill, PA 19444

Learn strategies to help your child cope with ADHD including "coaching"—a nontherapy support and encouragement process that provides the ADHD person with a coach to offer suggestions, boundaries and structure, teaching, listening, and, on occasion, constructive confrontation.

Learn about medical treatments and behavior management interventions used for ADHD.

Encourage the child to take part in Bible study groups (small-group studies) and to look for ways God provides His strength in our times of weakness.

Persons with Physical Disabilities

Nothing says "welcome to our church" like visible evidence. If a visitor can clearly see a place to park and an easy-to-enter entrance, she feels less hesitant to come in. Nothing says "welcome" like a building that is accessible to persons with physical disabilities.

I was reminded of that. Our downtown church serves many nonchurch children during the Vacation Bible School week. It was the parent night of VBS, and one third-grade girl was anxious to show her parents around. The mother looked at the two-story design and asked, "Where's the elevator?"

I turned to see the woman sitting in a wheelchair next to their van in the disabled parking spot. I quickly directed the family up a ramp, through the ground-level entry to the elevator which was located in a visible, main corridor of the building. I could tell by the look on the mother's face she was impressed with the accessibility.

Many churches and public-service buildings are now aware of the architectural barriers that keep persons with physical disabilities from coming into that building. Most new building codes require accommodations for wheelchairs and other orthopedic aids. Churches with older buildings can take surveys to determine how available their building is for persons with physical disabilities who want to take part in church activities. That may include basics such as: reserved parking, wider halls and doors, accessible rest rooms, curb cuts, ramps, and elevators. The survey, "How Accessible Is Your Church" is included in the Appendix. Use it to evaluate your church building.

Physically disabled persons should have access to all parts of the church. Ask a person in a wheelchair to assist in evaluating the accessibility of all areas of your church building. After you complete the survey:

1. Share and evaluate the results with church members.
2. Set goals to remove barriers.
3. Publicize and celebrate each goal.
4. Publicize your church's accessibility with the International Wheelchair logo in the newspaper, Yellow Pages™ ads, in church brochures, on your church sign.

Department rooms should be located and arranged for easy access and maneuverability. Make certain there is enough room to maneuver around the furniture with a wheelchair or other mobility aid. Rest rooms should be located as close to the room as possible.

Wheelchairs need to fit underneath tables, or lap boards need to be provided. Shelves, drawers, sinks, hangers, or hooks should be within easy reach. Floors should be made of slip-resistant materials that wheelchairs, scooters, and walkers can maneuver on easily and that provide shock absorbency.

Provide adaptive equipment such as cornerseats, wedges, bolsterseats. Check resource catalogs for the varied and new assistive devices on the market that allow children who cannot use their legs or sit without support to move, sit, or stand on their own. Your state's Pediatric Technology Program is willing to provide a list of service providers who are knowledgeable about fitting needs with the newest technology. Check your state's listing of federally-funded services to the handicapped. Satisfied parents and other customers can recommend suppliers of other rehabilitative equipment. Because many of these devices are expensive, check with local parent support groups for funding ideas or ways that devices can be constructed at less expense.

Adaptive materials

Provide the following resources:

- double-ring scissors for the member whose coordination demands extra help when cutting.
- lap boards, or trays with raised edges.
- pencil, crayon, or marker grips.
- suction grips to help the member steady himself.
- glue sticks.
- communication boards or electronic devices.
- adapted switches that permit easy use of battery-powered and electronic devices.

- materials taped to the table top or secured with Velcro.™

Teaching

Unless the member has additional disabilities, she does not require different teaching procedures from her age-group peers. You can adapt for her needs with these guidelines:

- Know about her disability. Read. Ask professionals. Ask the person or her parents. Don't be afraid to ask questions.
- Learn about any assistive equipment she may use.
- Make certain she is positioned comfortably and properly. Learn how to position her properly from her, her parents, or a therapist. Positioning refers to the assistance the member may need to lie down, sit, or stand comfortably and still best use her abilities. Proper positioning gives postural support and allows her to take part in the activity without worry. A properly positioned person has better control of her movements. Professionals say proper positioning helps to improve circulation, breathing, and digestion. Each disability will have its own positioning requirements. Positioning may be as simple as providing a different type of chair or a pillow, or as complex as knowing how to arrange a member at a body-support table.
- Know the member may need more time to complete an activity.
- Never do for a physically disabled person what she can do for herself.
- Accept the disability while focusing on the individual person and his strengths.
- Encourage him to use his talents and gifts.
- Don't equate physical disabilities with mental disabilities.
- Talk directly to her. Respect her level of understanding. *Do not* talk down to her.
- Know that a person who has become physically disabled as a result of an injury or illness deals with stress and grief. Minister to that person's level in the grieving process.

Physical Disabilities and Children

Many children with physical disabilities need positioning assistance. Teachers of children should be aware of the considerations parents face when they purchase positioning equipment.

1. What are the child's individual needs? Often a team of therapists, rehabilitation technologists, and the child's doctor decide what she requires based on her everyday activities. Some children can get help from a household item such as a box or pillow. Others may need complex positioning systems that require several pieces of specialized equipment. Specialized equipment is usually quite costly.
2. Where do we buy the equipment? Can we get it off the shelf, or is it a customized order? For how long can this one piece provide help for my child?
3. Can one piece serve dual purposes?
4. Is it user-friendly and easy to manipulate? Is it too heavy for the caregiver to lift? Is it easy to store or fold? Is it sturdy and reliable?
4. Does it meet the child's specific safety needs?
5. How are we going to pay for it? How soon will we need to spend that much money again?

Some children require the use of car seats and strollers even when they get older and heavier. Their positioning needs get complex, expensive, and harder to manage. The teacher's awareness of these issues can be helpful to parents as can a directory of rehabilitation suppliers (contact physical therapists at your local hospital for catalog resources) and a list of hospitals and suppliers who will let parents test equipment before they buy.

The Americans with Disabilities Act (ADA) requires that all public accommodations be accessible to persons with disabilities. This includes recreational areas and playgrounds. Your church can make certain that church playgrounds and equipment meet accessibility standards.

Paths to the equipment should be wide enough for a wheelchair (at least 60 inches) with surfaces that allow for easy maneuvering, such as rubber mats, rubber tiles, wood chips (thick and deep), or poured rubber-like surfaces that allow for shock absorbency in case of a fall.

Wheelchair ramps leading to equipment should have rails and raised edges to prevent a wheelchair or scooter from slipping off the sides. Make certain the slope of the ramp meets safety guidelines.

Accessible equipment includes: overhead rings and bars low enough so a child can reach them from a wheelchair; bridges; accessible slides which have paths with proper surfaces and transfer points that are raised platforms where a child can get out of her wheelchair or scooter and get onto the equipment; swings that provide body support (the sling swing); and elevated sandboxes children in wheelchairs and scooters can roll up to.

Accessible equipment should be integrated with standard equipment to encourage interaction between children with disabilities and their nondisabled peers. Have separate play areas for different age groups. Separate the preschool area from the one for children 6 to 12 years of age.

Follow general safety precautions: (1) fences with gates should surround the play area, especially if it is located near a street or parking lot; (2) play areas should be clean and free of trash and debris; and (3) supervision should be provided during all play times with at least two teachers present.

Playground safety specialists and commercial play-systems companies, along with parents, have done so much in recent years to create and develop accessible play equipment for children with physical disabilities. If your church playground is not accessible, involve parent support groups and community organizations to help you plan and even fund a play area that meets accessibility standards. Yours may be the only one in your community. Such a feature says "welcome" to the family of a child with physical disabilities.

Persons Who Are Gifted

A sincere and honest young woman told our conference group: "I came to this conference to learn about ADHD. I thought that might be my son's problem. But now I see that David is not hyper; he is just bored with church. He is five years old and reads third- and fourth-grade books. And he was showing me how to work simple addition problems last week. None of our activities seem to please him. Of course, we are a small church, and I have all children ages three to six in the same class for both Sunday School and Discipleship Training. David causes trouble with other children and doesn't like to take part in group activities. It isn't that he can't. He won't. And he doesn't respond to authority well, either. I pray for the days he doesn't come. Of course, that is not often. His dad is our pastor."

Many in the group could identify with that mother's frustration. They had met children like David, too. It didn't take long for the group to share suggestions and strategies they had used in similar situations. Everyone agreed David had a difficult time fitting in with his age-group peers because of his disability. From the indications given, David is probably a gifted child.

Persons who are gifted:

- have significantly above-average intelligence and talents that require special attention to nurture and develop.
- require specific ideas for teaching that encourage them to come to church and to grow spiritually.
- exhibit characteristics as varied as their personalities.
- display academic superiority in all areas, or they are specifically talented in one area.

Some gifted people exhibit an interest in the ideas and thoughts of others. They seem to know themselves well and accept themselves for who they are besides being gifted. Some gifted people wear their abilities like a badge and have a difficult time knowing and learning compassion for others. Some perform well in any area they choose.

Not all gifted persons are a joy to work with. Some cause trouble in class because they are not being challenged. Other gifted people quietly resign themselves to the boredom, but they do not stay long with the situation. This can cause teachers to feel frustrated and that they are not doing an adequate job of teaching the person.

Gifted people do not:
- fit any stereotype.
- always make straight A's.
- avoid sports and physical fitness activities.
- always have their noses in a book.
- always think they are smart.
- develop their potential without encouragement.
- know everything, nor do they have the capacity to learn everything.
- are not always introverted.

Persons who are truly gifted display rapid learning in early childhood. They can give long spans of attention to topics that interest them. They are quick to see how that topic relates to their lives or another topic, which is part of their ability to quickly grasp cause-effect relationships. That is one reason ordinary, routine things bore them quickly. Teachers of gifted children point out their students often do not have time to worry about their immediate environment. It is not unusual for gifted children to be cluttered and unorganized with their work because gifted persons display a high degree of curiosity. They are frequently involved in a variety of projects at one time. Gifted persons are more likely to be well-informed on a variety of topics. Their problem-solving abilities enable them to take facts (the general) and apply those concepts (the specific). Because gifted persons expect much from themselves and others, they are often most interested in social topics such as social reform, politics, and religion.

In the church, realize that persons who are gifted:
- do not readily accept "pat" answers.
- see outside the lines of traditions.
- ask challenging questions.
- need to be encouraged to develop spiritually inquiring minds.
- need to hear the spiritual inadequacy of all persons is met in the person of Jesus Christ.

Thinking and learning are hard work, even for a bright mind. A person who is intellectually bright has the potential to think deeply. She also has the potential to influence, encourage, and lead others. Because some gifted persons are not encouraged to develop their gifts at church and because they do not get the answers they seek, the individuals may give up on Christianity for their spiritual quests and leave the church.

"I hated having teachers who got offended at my questions. They acted mad at

me for being smart. I guess it made them uncomfortable."—Sarah, age 20

"I didn't like the class at first because all the guys wanted to spend their time talking about this one girl. I happened to know her at school, and I knew her reputation wasn't the best. But there was one other guy in the class who wanted to know more about the Bible, too. Our teacher worked so hard to make the class interesting for me and the other guy that I kept going back."—Kyle, age 16

"I have a hard time with the way the church excludes people who are different. I don't mean that I have been rejected here. It's just that people who don't have the clothes, or money to do everything, or who come from troubled families aren't as accepted here as they should be. I've tried to express my concerns, but I don't think people take me seriously. I get the impression they think I have strange ideas because I'm an artist."—Michelle, young adult

"As a teen, I had questions and concerns I now realize my youth leaders were not equipped to answer. At the time, I thought they were rejecting me and my ideas. I decided I would be out of there during college. I didn't have time for the church or the things of God. I'm glad God allowed me to meet other Christians on campus who eagerly welcomed my inquiries and gave me open, honest answers. I'm grateful for the abilities I have to serve God."—Mel, young adult

Do know it is not easy being gifted. Gifted children, youth, and adults experience frustration and confusion because they live in a world where others do not understand the way they think or the motivation and drive behind the things they do. Gifted people, especially children, have trouble developing close friendships. They are not readily accepted because their thoughts run ahead of their peers. At times, expectations put on gifted persons are too simple and therefore, cause discouragement. Other times expectations can be too much, bringing overwhelming demands. Often gifted persons feel distanced from the average world.

Persons who are gifted want:
- to be accepted and affirmed.
- to have honest responses, not simplistic explanations.
- to be heard concerning their thoughts, dreams, frustrations, and questions.
- to put their gifts to work.
- to know why it makes more sense to have a life committed to God.

Adaptations
Adaptations need to be made for persons who are gifted.
- Welcome questions without being threatened. If you don't have an answer, say so.
- Encourage the member to design a Bible-learning project relating to his question.
- Provide books and resource materials for use outside of class that speak to the biblical or historical content of the question.
- Appoint study teams to investigate a topic.
- Use the member's ability to articulate through writing, music, or other creative forms.
- Encourage him to express the *whys* and *hows* of an issue or topic.
- Offer choices. Plan a learning environment that allows freedom to study.
- Ask your own thought-provoking questions that address concepts and real-life applications.
- Encourage problem solving by using analogies, comparisons, brainstorming, and creative thinking.
- Encourage talented members to share their talents, but don't pressure.
- Provide leadership roles: outreach-evangelism leader, care leader, assistant teacher, peer

tutoring, Youth Ministry Council member.
- Use creative teaching techniques such as drama, creative writing, puzzles, or game-show formats that keep the member interested and involved.

In short, do not allow the challenges of the bright mind to intimidate you. Look for the member's learning strengths and develop the opportunities to turn those challenges toward the bright mind in ways that will stimulate and interest him or her.

I treasure the year my daughter had Linda as a teacher. Tall. Elegant. Wise. That's how I've remembered Linda all these years. She was also quite gifted intellectually, as were her husband and their two children. Linda knew how to motivate and encourage my gifted child. But she knew more. She knew how to encourage the gifts in all her students. In the Christian-school setting, Linda was free to say: "God has given each of you talents and gifts for His glory. I want to help you develop those talents." Linda often said, "All children are gifted." She accepted her superior intellect with humility and used it to help others feel good about themselves. I am thankful my child was influenced by a gifted person like Linda.

While thinking about the talents and gifts of bright minds, remember the gifts and talents of all your members. Never forget brothers and sisters may be gifted in different ways, so never compare a child's accomplishments to those of the brighter sibling. Encourage each of your members to develop their talents and gifts. Look for ways to affirm each member and plan for each member to have time in the spotlight as she shares her thoughts and abilities.

Help persons with leadership potential know how to serve. Gifted persons may often show a promise of leadership, but so do other members. Use case studies of biblical characters, great names in church history, and profiles of people in your community to help members see that a good leader first knows how to serve others.

Avoid giving the gifted member preferential treatment. This can cause other members to resent him. Provide opportunities for positive social interaction between the gifted member and his peers.

Since gifted persons are potential leaders and policymakers of the future, help them focus on knowing and pleasing God; learn to evaluate their strengths and improve their weaknesses; and learn that even when we cannot control or answer all of life's mysteries we can control our own responses to circumstances and to God.

Persons with Autism

Autism refers to a wide variety of abnormal behaviors that appear by the time a child is three years of age. These behaviors can include rejection of all physical contact, continual body movement, or an extreme compulsion to order the immediate environment. Autistic behaviors can also include heightened sensations such as hearing or diminished sensations such as pain.

Professionals identify as many as 40 symptoms associated with autism. Some of these include:
- little or no eye contact.
- reversal of the pronouns *you* and *me*.
- unusual knowledge in one specific area or difficulty naming objects.
- fixation on spinning objects, on words or numbers, on sameness.
- rejection of cuddling and touching from others.
- not speaking or merely mimicking sounds.
- bizarre facial expressions or total lack of facial expression.
- lack of social interaction; no interest in playing with other children;

inappropriate social interactions.
- body-rocking, hand-flipping, head-banging movements.
- unreasonable resistance to changes in his routine or in the way he orders his room or environment.
- extreme responses to sounds, odors, or pain that may cause him to become physically aggressive to others or himself; unusual fear of harmless, everyday objects, but little or no fear of real danger.

A child diagnosed with autism will have several of these behaviors. Some children exhibit a few autistic-type behaviors, but they are not diagnosed as being truly autistic. A large number of persons with autism are also mentally retarded, but some people are both autistic and gifted.

Depending on the degree of the behaviors, most persons with autism respond best to a behavior-modification treatment.

At church, the child with autism can often be mainstreamed with her age-group peers. Give her genuine acceptance.

Follow a consistent schedule. It helps to display a poster in the room that tells or pictures the schedule. If you need to make changes in the schedule or the arrangement of the room, explain them to her before the session begins. You can avoid confusion for her if you will explain what is going to happen next and what she is expected to do.

Use simple sentences. The autistic child has delays in language development and communication skills, both verbal and nonverbal. Give directions in positive, short, clear sentences.

Provide clues. The child with autism often displays an inability to draw a conclusion from information. She has difficulty with directions and understanding jokes.

Give her concrete and real-life learning activities. Because of her language deficits, she learns best with visual and tactual senses.

Provide opportunities for him to interact with nondisabled peers so he can see how to play with other children and with toys.

Provide one-on-one activities and frequent activity changes for her short attention span.

Maintain open communication with her parents and school teachers to provide consistency between home, school, and church.

As a youth or adult with autism develops, he often becomes more social and able to interact. Within the past 20 years the number of persons institutionalized because of autism has dropped dramatically. Studies show that with early childhood treatment and consistent management many persons with autism improve enough to function in society, and a large number seem to be cured. Adults who have overcome autistic habits explain the isolation of the autistic world:

"It is a world of silence."
"It is feeling bad about myself all the time."
"I felt like I was all wrong all the time."
"On occasion I still experience anxiety and fear that I will return to that world."

The church family is an ideal group to help the person with autism learn correct social interactions and to emerge from the isolation of autism by providing:
- loving and caring responses.
- role models of appropriate social interactions.
- opportunities to learn how to say hello and good-bye appropriately.
- encouragement when progress seems slow or nonexistent.
- opportunities to build the senses of person, self-worth, value, and belonging,
- fellowship.

Fred was a example of an older adult with autism who often repeats a word or phrase. For Fred it was, "What time is it?" He asked me that so often I can still hear the exact way he'd slide it all out, "Wh't ti-i-i-me is i-i-i-t?" He'd always extend his pocket watch, which he kept in perfect running order, hoping I would say, "I don't know. What does your watch say?"

I learned Fred was born to older-age parents 50 years before. His dad could get Fred to respond to him only when he asked that same question. Possibly Fred needed another question to ask.

So I began to tell him, "When you see me, you need to ask, 'How are you?' I will answer that question. Then you can show me your watch." It took a few months before Fred remembered to ask me the correct question without prompts. Fred eventually learned to use that same greeting with other people. I knew little about autism at that time. I only knew I got tired of hearing the same question over and over.

More About Mainstreaming

I am fascinated with the magnitude of the Mississippi River. The power and depth in a large river or an ocean fill me with awe and fear. Even though I love to swim, or maybe because I do, I have a healthy respect for the potential in water to both help and destroy.

One thing I have noticed about the Mississippi—she can get so full that she bursts out of her seams, but she never refuses to accept the water that channels into her banks. She cannot stop to evaluate and select from the streams and rivers that empty into her. It is not a part of her nature. There is no pecking order, no hierarchy of importance. There is water from the west, water from the east. Once water flows into the Mississippi that water becomes the Mississippi, moving along the river's course, sometimes tumbling and turning over the rocks, heading toward the Gulf. Talk about a literal main stream!

Ideally, that is how the church should be—one big awesome body with the potential to change lives through the power of God. Ideally no pecking order, no one person more "right" to join ranks than another should be the normal course. Once a person chooses to be a part of God's church, he or she becomes God's church moving through life, sometimes tumbling and turning over the rocks of earthly life, heading toward eternal life. That's an example of mainstream.

Realistically, this is not the way it happens. Consciously or unconsciously, in our churches we do make selections. We often assume the people who join with us will be like us. We all do that. Some of us have our predetermined expectations—whole bodies and whole minds make whole spirits. We forget our bodies and minds are separate entities from our spirits. Whole bodies and whole minds can mean disabled spirits. Disabled bodies and exceptional minds can equal wholly restored spirits. We forget the spirit inside each human being is the part that is made in God's image.

Just this week, I read an article about a worship service in the great Central Baptist Church in Moscow, Russia. This beautiful, historical church managed to stay open during the Communist era. Its pews and balconies, aisles and vestibule are filled with devoted people who appreciate the privilege of worship. They have experienced the horror and terror of not having much of anything. Of course, I read the color picture before I read the article. I studied the serious faces of the congregation. I noticed the large crowd and the beauty of the architecture. I saw the preacher and speakers perched high on the pulpit balcony. Then my eye was drawn to the elevated platform below the pulpit. Sitting in her chair, with a traditional scarf tied around her head, was an interpreter for deaf people. Here was an

example in a missions magazine of a place for everyone!

The entire scene struck me. These are my brothers and sisters in Jesus Christ, so appreciative of the opportunity to worship they will sit or stand through a two-hour service. These are people of prayer who have endured suffering for their faith that I do not comprehend. And they made preparations for people who are hearing impaired. No selfishness or lack of forethought there. I wondered, *Which of them is physically disabled or mentally handicapped? I know they must be in there some place.* It seems right to expect that as this crowd pushes into place, it makes a place for everyone who channels into her banks.

Just like the mighty Mississippi River.

---

[1]From the Holy Bible, *New International Version*, copyright © 1973, 1978, 1984 by International Bible Society. Subsequent quotations are marked NIV

[2]Order these materials from Customer Service Service, 127 Ninth Avenue, North, Nashville, Tennessee 37234-0113; FAX (615) 251-5933; or e-mail to CompuServe ID 70423,2526.

Q&A

Complete this sentence: Just as we use _____ in all types

of study, we need to use a _____ base about
the needs of exceptional persons in all types of ministry.

Define mainstreaming: _____

_____

_____

_____

In what ways do you think mainstreaming provides the church with increased
outreach into the community?

_____

_____

List three examples of successful integration strategies:

1. _____

2. _____

3. _____

What is your primary learning style? How can knowing about learning styles help you
be a more effective teacher?

_____

_____

Choose one of the exceptionalities discussed in this chapter. What other things do you
want to know about it? List a resource in your own community where you can obtain
more information about it.

_____

_____

A Place for Caring

A place for caring:
- invites persons with disabilities to minister.
- seeks to minister to all families, including single-parent and adoptive families.
- provides opportunities to meet needs in practical ways.
- develops a Person/Family-Centered Plan to coordinate efforts to meet those needs.

When I was in college, Donna told me about Jerry and her brother. I didn't understand it then. Why would a man recently returned from the war in southeast Asia want to do that? Jerry and Donna were merely friends; they didn't even date each other.

Donna said, "Jerry goes to my parents' house one night each week to stay with Brother so my parents can go out to dinner, shop, or go to a movie."

I didn't understand the significance of what she said. Donna patiently explained, "Brother is 23 years old. He has severe handicaps. He is mentally retarded, and he can't move much.

He likes Jerry to come over and watch TV with him. Brother needs constant care. My parents and I have been tied down to him all his life, so we really appreciate Jerry's willingness to help."

I didn't know much about multiple disabilities and respite care then, but I did recognize an act of caring. This one simple commitment served more than one person. Even my life was influenced by it.

This chapter is about caring, helping, and serving. I cannot begin to cover all there is to know about caring for persons with disabilities, but first consider individual needs. This is the basis for caring. Then develop strategies to meet those needs.

I want to encourage you to help and serve others as you go through life. While you are going, make it a habit to give and receive help and service in an unpretentious manner. Plan not to take double-size portions on your plate. Small, bite-size pieces of caring that you can accomplish without burnout are far more effective than elaborate programs.

Who should care?—The pastor and church staff are not the only people who should care. All believers are called to care. Indeed, all church members are encouraged to care.

What do you do when you care?—To care means to help or serve others. It means to offer aid and accommodate. It can mean to wait on someone and watch over him or her.

How do you care?—A spirit of caring is shown by being a Sunday School teacher; by being a choir member; by visiting shut-ins; through writing or composing; being a preacher; or by being a prayer warrior.

These are good examples of what you might do through your church or vocation. How do you care in your everyday walk through life? How do you encourage other people to care? What other caring ministries can you offer in or through your church?

Accept Caring from Persons with Disabilities

A place for caring is a place where persons with disabilities can help, care, and serve. Those persons provide unique perspectives of wisdom and spiritual insights. They are effective team players and capable partners for the sake of the gospel.

That may be a change in thinking for you. We are conditioned to think about the things we can do for those with a greater disability than our own. We think we should wait on them, watch over them. We have made them dependent on us. That concept limits the amount of work we can get done for the sake of God's kingdom. It takes away from the disabled person's dignity and sense of worth. Caring is a give-and-take relationship. This section deals with the ability of persons who are disabled to give of themselves, using their unique gifts and abilities.

Persons with more involved disabilities are enhancing the work force in all areas of society every day. We need to tap into this pool of talent. Whatever the skills, abilities, or limits, a place for everyone means that caring is our responsibility. We get equal shares of blessing for being ministers.

Persons with disabilities want to be included in the caring of the church. They are asking for the opportunity. Nondisabled people seek partners in the caring of the church. They should intentionally seek opportunities for persons with disabilities to provide that help.

When we are trying to get a job done, we often fail to see the hidden talent sitting in our small groups and pews. We overlook a large resource of qualified persons who can help and serve with us.

Many people with disabilities have made a positive impact on our lives. They are a testimony of the way God works His plan through individuals. They encourage us to ask God to send more people like them.

What can persons with disabilities do? Anything their talents allow. Try this. In a five-minute time limit, list all persons with disabilities who have ministered to you in some way. Stay within the time limit. Don't forget to include one-time encounters or small children. Compare your list to my list.

Your List

_____

_____

_____

_____

_____

_____

_____

_____

_____

_____

_____

My List

A woman who was physically disabled in her legs and feet because she contracted typhoid fever as a teen

A person who was visually impaired as a result of a childhood head injury

A preacher who lost one arm in World War II

An evangelist who uses a wheelchair

A pastor who is intellectually gifted

A lady with cerebral palsy who told me: "I love the song 'Oh, How I Love Jesus.' He loves me when others reject me."

A young boy with multidisabilities whose trust and obedience for his daddy model the way I should trust and obey my heavenly Father.

Two gifted and talented editors who encourage and teach me

A retired missionary overly blessed with talents and abilities who, in spite of a lifelong illness, ministers to all of us with her sense of humor.

My friend who allows life-threatening scleroderma (a disease that causes hardening of the skin and organ systems) to teach her about God's goodness.

Dozens of adults with mental handicaps who love me

Persons with disabilities are ministering all around us. They are like you and me, wanting to use their abilities for God. They can use their abilities in the following ways.

- As small-group leaders sharing from personal life experiences and difficulties the spiritual principles and answers God has taught them.
- In genuine relationships as they share with others what it means to be a follower of Jesus Christ.
- In music and drama to help others express worship.
- In prayer groups or prayer chains.
- On church planning committees.
- As class outreach-evangelism leaders.
- As pastors, ministers of education, music ministers.
- By their presence.

Persons with mental disabilities should be encouraged to take part in ministry opportunities. Adults in their separate department can do many things to care for one another.

Susan remembers each member's and teacher's birthday with a thoughtfully selected card.

Stanley comes to church early each Sunday to make coffee and help arrange his department room.

Damon rides the van each Sunday to help with friends who have problems getting on and off the van.

Erma prays for her teacher and class members.

Ruth was one of the first members of our class for adults with mental disabilities. Her disabilities were the result of a stroke and the brain tumor that eventually killed her. Her history fascinated me. She raised nine children, mostly as a single mom. She drove a truck and a cab in a large metropolitan city to earn money. Even though her children were grown, she still managed to help them on her disability salary. Ruth was a new Christian when we met, and I've never seen another person appreciate Jesus Christ like she did. She encouraged and prayed for me. She helped me see God in a way I never knew before. We knew her prognosis was not encouraging, and I prayed that when it was her time to die God would take her gently, and He did. In her life and death she ministered to me.

Adults in their separate department can do many things to serve the church body.

They can serve as greeters in worship service.

They can serve as ushers.

They can serve on churchwide cleanup days.

They can serve by taking care of a small flower garden.

They can serve by taking part in visitation.

They can serve by praying for the pastor and church staff.

They can serve by folding church bulletins.

They can serve by placing hymnals in the pew racks after church or helping to pick up cups after the Lord's Supper.

They can serve by active participation in the worship service.

Adults and children with multiple disabilities, persons who do not speak, who may not walk or even move much, are able to bring a dimension of spiritual teaching to our lives in ways no other person can. Have you ever looked into the eyes of a multidisabled child and seen the dignity of the human spirit? Have you ever encountered the warmth of a truly kind smile? Do you know what it feels like to be genuinely accepted? Have you watched as a nonverbal person with limited mobility praises God?

I recently met two men. One is actually a 17-year-old who weighs about 60

pounds. He has cerebral palsy and rides in a sling-back stroller. He is nonverbal, but I know he understands much of what I say to him. He has beautiful brown eyes, and he likes to high five with me. When he comes to worship service, I think he enjoys the music, but he probably doesn't understand much of the preaching. I don't know what he thinks about God except that he is familiar with the word.

The other man, a father of grown children, works hard to keep his body strong and fit and is quite intelligent and articulate. He possibly has more head knowledge about God than I ever will. When it comes to worship, he likes the music, is attentive about the preaching, and exhibits a truly loving heart for God.

I have watched both of them in worship service and wondered if the older man is more important there than the younger. Which of these men brings more joy to the heart of God? Is one more valuable than the other? God loves them both because He is the Creator. My young friend helps me understand that God loves me, not because of the things I do, but because He chooses to love me. That gives me peace. By his presence, my young friend ministers to me.

Offer Caring to Persons Who Are Disabled and to Their Families

Part of caring is willingness to be involved in the lives of other people. A place for everyone offers authentic sharing and caring to persons with disabilities and to their families.

Families of persons with disabilities have needs you and your church can help to meet. Authentic caring in these cases means having sensitive and practical responses to harsh realities.

Families of exceptional persons tend to be skeptical and must know that any ministry of the church is genuine and ongoing, that it is more than a "do-good" smoke screen that quickly fades and disperses. Disabilities are long-term. Caring must be a long-term accomplishment.

Offer Caring to Families

Families of disabled persons identify problems in one or more of these areas:
- social isolation and limited friendships.
- lack of support and understanding.
- physical exhaustion.
- marital problems.
- financial burdens.
- grief, anger, and resentment.
- spiritual questions, hurts, and frustrations.
- concerns about the future.

Church members can be the friends and extended family for these families in practical ways. The pressures of raising a child with disabilities or living with a family member who has suddenly become disabled are complex and painful. The emotional drains and the financial and physical strains can be devastating.

Families are often tired of comments and questions. They are certainly tired of clichés and spiritual explanations for the disruptions in their lives. It can be the same for a family with a gifted member or a family with a person who has multiple disabilities. Barriers rise that keep these families from coming to church or being with Christian friends.

Barriers can be broken down by establishing a climate of acceptance throughout the church. Barrier-breaking is something pastors and church staff model for adult church members, who in turn model it for youth and children. Acceptance is a result of breaking down fears with facts and education.

Caring for families means making an effort to respond to the needs of individual members in the family. In addition to other concerns, family members frequently deal with resentments the pressures the disability put on the family. Families with an exceptional member do not want to make their pain public. They choose to hide it from fellow believers for fear of rejection.

Care for single-parent families.—As estimated 80 percent of marriages end in divorce when there is a disabled family member (especially a child). There are just so many pressures! Parents vacillate between being filled with guilt and putting the blame on the spouse's family for the problem. It is an embarrassing and frustrating situation, especially to fathers. Then, too, parents can become hostile and angry with God for their situation. Their spiritual barometers bottom out, and before long they find they have made destructive decisions. Most of the time, the mother receives full custody of the children.

Both mothers and fathers who have experienced this kind of divorce say the divorce is a terrible, tragic cataclysm. Siblings of the exceptional child are doubly hurt as they deal with additional responsibilities and grief. To many, the sense of loss is overwhelming.

Life with children and a spouse can be hectic enough. A single parent, especially if one of the children has special needs, will find life can be chaotic. Often maintaining some sense of structure and consistency is best for the family member who is disabled as well as all family members. An effective ministry to the single-parent family is a team-approach effort committed to helping each member of the family find healing and wholeness.

Care for adoptive families.—Couples wishing to adopt find the number of adoptable infants has decreased over the years. The demand is greater than the supply. Many unmarried women are keeping their babies rather than putting them up for adoption. Abortions also have contributed to fewer babies available for adoption.

Research and professionals suggest adoptive families are four times more likely to have a child with highly involved special needs than a birth family is. Several factors influence this statistic. Higher percentages of the birth mothers who choose to place the child for adoption do not have proper self-care and medical care during the pregnancy. Many adoptable babies are subject to fetal substance abuse.

Couples who yearn for a child take the risks in order to have a family. When they do adopt, the stresses and pains these families bear are both similar to, and yet unique from, those of a birth family. The amount of financial strain is even greater.

Some churches have been less sensitive to the needs and heartaches of adoptive parents than to birth parents of a disabled child. An adopted child with special needs is more likely to have severe and multiple handicapping involvement. The behaviors and limitations workers see are harder to deal with at church. More than a few adoptive parents report negative comments from their fellow church members about their choice to adopt such a child.

My friend and her husband adopted his niece when she was one year old. Even though they had two birth children, they wanted to provide the child with a loving home. The birth mother, who was abusive to the child and her siblings, was heavily into drug and other substance abuses. It wasn't until their daughter was seven or eight years old that the adoptive parents realized the extent of damage the birth mother's drug habits had on the child. Many experiences of raising her have been harsh and painful. The entire family has paid the price for reaching out to a hurt child. The problems have been compounded by the lack of understanding from people at the church. There have been a lot of criticisms but few, if any, offers for creative helps and service.

A place for everyone means churches like yours and mine need to share in the joys and trials of adoptive families. Such families with a disabled member deserve commendation and support from their church family.

Many Christian couples adopt because they take a stand against abortion. These families are doing something about a social problem many people ignore. Many times they adopt the children no one else wants. Often they love children who are not capable of showing love in return. They pay much in terms of time and money to model the love of Jesus Christ in a hurting world.

Care for families in purposeful ways.—The ministries you offer to families of disabled persons will be varied and unique to each situation. Some of these might include:

- marital counseling sessions or seminars.
- counseling for siblings.
- friendship, inviting family members home or to a recreational activity.
- small-group Bible studies.
- an evening at the theatre or a musical production.
- hobby and craft projects.
- coffee at a late-night cafe.
- genuine listening skills.
- learning all you can about the disability.
- offering to take persons shopping.
- making certain each member of the family can take part in the life of the church.
- advocacy for persons judged incapacitated.
- nontraditional ministries such as VBS for special-needs children, in-home studies for homebound persons, midweek Bible study classes, residential supports for those who want to live as independently as possible.
- extended service for older children or youth.
- weekend retreats for adults with mental disabilities.

Families with family members who are disabled can be cared for through support groups and with financial help.

Provide a network of Christian people to whom families with special needs can relate.—Among these networks can be support groups for parents of gifted children, parents of multidisabled children, patients with chronic illnesses, siblings of exceptional persons. Your church can volunteer its building one night each month for support groups. Provide childcare, if needed, and a light refreshment. Encourage deacons and church workers to attend any group that relates to the needs of a family in your church.

Many families with special needs sometimes find themselves in financial trouble. They need financial help.—Adaptive aids, special shoes, school programs, and medicine are some of the items families may need, but families find these items are too costly. A disability is usually a costly fact of life. This is a sensitive area, and many families with a disabled member are embarrassed about sharing these needs with others. Sunday School teachers, homebound workers, and deacons can work together to make needs known to the proper church committee or group. The church can work through the benevolence committee, ask for volunteer donations, or sponsor a fund-raising event. Handle meeting this type of need with care and discretion.

Single parents need support.—Usually the single parent of a disabled child is the mother. Even when a father shares custody, the additional strains on a mother's time and resources are draining. The single mother benefits from:

- a Sunday School class for single-again women or an age-group class.
- a network of persons who can help provide legal and financial advice.

- other couples who develop a relationship with the child and friends to go with her to school events.
- a singles department.
- automobile maintenance.
- respite care, baby-sitting services, an adult to sit with the children during church.

Both church and secular organizations see respite care as a great need for all families with an exceptional member.—Parents and family members need a break from care responsibilities on a regular basis. Relief time to family members has been provided successfully through:

- a team of adults trained to provide care service in the home for children and adults, including medically fragile persons.
- Parents Night Out sponsored once each month by the singles department of the church.
- adult daycare services.
- weekend activities such as a day-long retreat or a VBS.
- overnighters at a friend's house.
- homebound worker who goes into the home on Sunday mornings so the family can attend church services together.

Person/Family-Centered Plan

Schools, work centers, and some residential facilities are required to keep written plans and goals for each disabled consumer of that program. This is an idea that many churches have found wise to emulate. A written plan or strategy is a good idea in order:

- to provide for the total integration of families into the life of the church.
- to keep up with the progress and needs of church families that have an exceptional member.
- to form an easy method of information sharing.
- to regularly evaluate the ways the church ministers to the family.

One mission of the church is to equip all family members to develop and grow spiritually. Families with an exceptional member can participate more fully when the church conveys a clear message regarding the worth of the exceptional member. A Person/Family-Centered Plan helps workers try to understand what it is like to have a disabled family member. We see individuals, not stereotypes, and demonstrate authentic interests in the family's spiritual goals. Such a partnership creates effective ways to identify and focus on the most pressing areas of ministry. Breaking needs into more easily manageable goals builds encouragement and hope.

A Person/Family-Centered Plan includes writing individual learning goals for multidisabled children, forming teams of interested persons to ensure successful integration for an autistic youth, developing a Person/Family-Centered Plan for the deacons, providing informal networking among workers for information sharing.

General Guidelines for a Person/Family-Centered Plan
General guidelines can help your church develop a Person/Family-Centered Plan that meets the unique mix and blend of your members' needs.

1. Use a team approach. Include such people as Sunday School teacher(s), the family deacon, parent or other family member, the exceptional person (when appropriate), minister of education, division director, workers from other church programs.

2 Designate a team member to keep the pastor informed on the achievements and strategies of the plan.

3. Develop a written plan. It is wise to use the same form if there are several families or persons who would benefit from a Person/Family-Centered Plan. Keep the form as simple and uncluttered as possible.

4. File a written copy of the plan in the church office. Make a copy of the plan for each team member.

5. Review and update the Person/Family-Centered Plan at regular, either six-month or one-year, intervals. (Important! Be consistent with this.)

6. Choose either the division director, minister of education, or the deacon as team leader. His or her job will be to schedule and conduct team meetings.

An example plan is found in the Appendix. Try to keep information to one side of the page for easy use. You may use this idea or develop your own. Note that this plan addresses more than one need for the family.

Other Ideas for a Person/Family-Centered Plan

A Person/Family-Centered Plan may be needed for special situations. Write ministry goals for the suddenly disabled adult. These will include ways to help her through the grief process as well as define any necessary new teaching methods. Write individual learning goals for adults who live in group homes. Write internship programs and goals for gifted youth and career/college adults. Develop strategy plans for making the building accessible for senior adults.

Power Source

Caring people want to let God work through them. Caring for the sake of itself will be a fruitless burden. Before you begin any ministry, ask God to show you where you are to care for and serve others. Keep your focus on what God wants you to do. You will not help others if you are overloaded. Plug in to the power source.

Q& A

In a five-minute time limit, list all persons with disabilities who have ministered to you in some way.

_____

_____

_____

_____

Name a person with disabilities who is currently ministering in your church.

_____

_____

Study the Person/Family-Centered Plan in the Appendix. What changes would you make in it to fit your church's purposes?

_____

_____

_____

Describe one way you can minister to a family with a disabled child. If you don't know such a family, imagine one. Tell briefly about the family, describe one specific need they have, explain how you can minister to that need.

_____

_____

_____

_____

_____

A Place for Witnessing

A place for witnessing:
- shares God's love.
- expresses hope and a sense of worth for each individual.
- witnesses to unsaved persons with disabilities and their families.
- teaches persons with mental disabilities about baptism.
- offers church membership to persons with disabilities.

He stood to share his Christian testimony during a meeting on Wednesday evening. As a highly intelligent teen, he hungered for more than a nominal religion. Christianity had nothing to offer, he thought. He began to study all formal religions.

"I didn't want glib answers. I had a quick mind and finished high school sooner than usual. By the time I started college, it wasn't enough for me to read about a religion, I had to try it. I was especially drawn to the teachings of Buddha," he said.

With each experience, he became more disillusioned with religion. The longing remained, but he thought he would never find the answers. A friend persisted in inviting him to church.

"There was a sense of peace at the church; I saw it on people's faces. I was drawn to that peace and confidence. When the pastor preached, I realized my longings were spiritual, not intellectual. The Holy Spirit convicted me that what I had been searching for all those years was the love of God," he confessed.

The soul of every person hungers for a right relationship with God. Persons with disabilities especially need to hear about God's love.

Persons with disabilities, other than mental, and families and caregivers will be able to hear the gospel. They can accept or reject what they hear. The person sharing a personal testimony needs to include My Life Before Christ, How I Accepted Christ, and What God Is Doing in My Life Today.

This chapter concentrates on witnessing to unsaved persons who have mental disabilities and other persons with disabilities. Many people genuinely believe that persons with mental disabilities do not need to be saved. That is a false assumption. We do not know how much some of these persons understand about spiritual matters, but we do know God commands us to share the good news with *all* people. This chapter focuses on our obedience to God's command. What happens after that is the work of the Holy Spirit. General principles of witnessing given in this chapter can apply as we share Jesus Christ with persons who are disabled.

Share God's Love

Love is the basis for sharing our faith and witnessing to others. We share God's love because we have accepted His love and grace in our lives; the natural result of our salvation is to share it with others. We share God's love with persons with mental disabilities when we follow the pattern He gives us in 1 Corinthians 13. Love understands what the person can and cannot do. We express God's love through our kindness and thoughtful actions. God's love enables us to be happy about persons' accomplishments and victories.

Love prompts us to teach persons how to live in ways that please God. Love is given with no strings attached. We share God's love when we tell persons with mental disabilities God's love will never go away.

We can make these statements about God with assurance because the Bible says, "I will declare that your love stands firm forever, that you established your faithfulness in heaven itself" (Ps. 89:2, NIV).[1] "Many are the woes of the wicked, but the Lord's unfailing love surrounds the man who trusts in him" (Ps. 32:10, NIV).

God's love is the only thing that cannot be taken away from us. Persons with mental disabilities may lose their jobs, experience the loss of family and friends, have their

possessions stolen or destroyed, move to a new residential situation. But like the ancient psalmists and you and me, they want to know they can depend on God to love and care for them.

Following are some points to keep in mind when sharing your faith with a person who is mentally disabled.

1. *Acknowledge* the individual's presence. Let her know you are aware she is a person with individual characteristics and needs, including her disability.
2. *Accept* the person for the things you like about him. Accept the disability. Accept the things about the person you may not like. Accept your responsibility to deal with any negative responses you may feel toward the disability.
3. Assume she has worth. The value of all people was established by God at creation. *Affirm* that worth and value by the things you say and do.
   • Let her know she matters to you.
   • Be helpful in practical ways.
   • Speak to her respectfully and appropriately for her age and abilities.
   • Identify her strengths and tell her she blesses your life.
   • Ask and answer questions and engage in genuine communication.
4. *Admit* God loved him enough to send His Son to die for him. Let him know you love him because God first loved you.
5. *Abide in* the hope that comes from knowing God. It is not a hope that disillusions, that says if we believe in God He'll make the disability go away. It's a hope that assures us there is more to life than this present age or the state of the body, a hope which results from the joy of our confidence that God is Sovereign over eternity. He walks with us now; He will walk with us in dark days to come. He will welcome us home for all eternity. This hope gives an entirely different perspective as we live our lives today.

Share Your Faith

Look for opportunities to share your faith. Begin by praying for unsaved people with mental disabilities who are in your community. Pray for their families and caregivers.

Develop and participate in outreach activities designed to cultivate relationships with unsaved persons with mental disabilities. Offer a Bible study, enroll the unsaved, encourage them to study God's Word.

Teach the Bible. Lay foundations for understanding salvation with the truths and principles from God's Word. Build on this foundation for Christian conversion and spiritual growth. As appropriate, give an evangelistic emphasis to the Bible study session.

Pray and prepare to share the good news of salvation. Witness to unsaved persons and their families as the Holy Spirit directs and leads you. Look for signs of readiness. Often persons with mental disabilities will alert you to their readiness by the questions they ask about baptism, going forward during the invitation, death, why Jesus came to earth, what heaven is like. As persons show signs of readiness, schedule a time to talk with them privately.

Many times persons want to talk as soon as Sunday School is dismissed. Plan how you will answer questions and share. The following suggestions may help you as you seek to tell someone about God's love.

1. Start with the Bible. Use a simplified version the person is able to understand.
2. Share Bible verses that are relevant to each individual. Simplify the verses into phrases to help the person understand.
3. Avoid using abstract phrases—"Ask Jesus into your heart" and "Be born again." Persons

with mental disabilities do not understand these terms.

4. Know how to define words so the person can understand. Use these suggestions or prepare your own: *sin*—doing wrong things; *punishment*—the action that happens because we have done something wrong; *forgive*—letting go of anger, not staying mad for what has been done; *sorry*—knowing I do not want to do wrong. I want to be forgiven; *believe*—know that Jesus took the punishment for me so God can forgive me.

5. Know what you are going to say:

   God loves you very much (John 3:16).

   Everyone sins and does wrong things. (Rom. 3:23).

   God sent Jesus to die and take the punishment for the wrong things you did. God raised Jesus from death (1 Cor. 15:3-4).

   You must make a choice to believe in Jesus or not (John 3:36).

   You must tell God your choice (1 John 4:15).

   You should share your new belief with others (Matt. 28:19-20).

6. Use the tone of voice you would use when talking to an adult. Do not talk down to the person.

7. After you share biblical truths, do not pressure the person into making a choice. Let the Holy Spirit bring about conviction. Don't ask such questions as: Do you want to go to heaven? Do you want Jesus to be your Friend? Avoid questions the person can answer with *yes*. She is most likely to answer in the way she thinks will please you, not from her own convictions or choices.

8. Pray with another teacher or class member that God will help the person choose to accept Jesus Christ as his Savior.

9. Speak with parents or guardians about the conversation. If you know they are Christians, ask for their support and prayer. If you know they are not Christians, briefly explain the person's questions and your responses. By doing so, you are sharing your faith with the parents or caregivers, too. They will appreciate your consideration of keeping them informed about their family member.

When the person decides to make a public profession of her acceptance of Jesus Christ, plan to meet her at the front of the church. Walk down the aisle with her only if she comes and asks you to do so. Let the initiative be on her part.

Patrick came to me after Sunday School. Not only was I his teacher, but also I am his court-appointed legal guardian. He wanted to talk with me about going forward during the invitation. I wanted to make certain he understood what he was asking. I asked why he wanted to go forward.

"To talk to the preacher; I want to join the church," he said.

I talked with Patrick about his own personal faith in Jesus. Patrick told me that, one recent Sunday in church, he had asked God to forgive his sins. He had been thinking about baptism since then. I asked Patrick to think about it two more weeks. If he still thought he should make a public profession of faith, he would remember to come to me. He did.

Two weeks later, after Sunday School, he said: "I am ready to talk to the preacher today."

We talked and prayed. I knew Patrick was certain of his salvation. I told him to go by himself during the invitation, and I would meet him there. He did it. He explained it all to the pastor. One thing you should understand about Patrick; he is a person with Down syndrome, labeled severely mentally handicapped. That didn't stop the Holy Spirit from working in his life.

We want our Sunday School class members to be received and welcomed in church. We do not want them to draw negative attention to themselves. Sharing

God's love with them includes helping them learn appropriate ways to behave in church. Use these strategies to help.

- Talk with the entire class at regular intervals about the meaning of the invitation. Encourage members to talk with you if they feel directed to go forward.
- Talk with the pastor and with all decision counselors ahead of time. Explain that you will watch for your members who go forward during the invitation. You will come to the front to help counsel them.
- What about the person with mental disabilities who walks the aisle every Sunday? Tell counselors and the pastor there may be times when members like the positive attention they get from going forward the first time. Say that when the member comes forward again, you and he can go quietly to a room outside the worship center. Try to keep the attention given him at a minimum. If the behavior continues, find out what is actually bothering him. Explain that God will forgive us any moment of the day. We don't need to save up our confessions for Sunday mornings.
- It may be that the person wants to share his prayer requests. Arrange for him to meet with his deacon or a teacher before the worship service begins.
- If necessary, explain to the member the inappropriateness of going forward all the time. If he lives with his parents, ask them to support you in helping to change the behavior.

Baptism

After the person with mental disabilities has made a profession of faith in Jesus Christ, counsel her, her parents, and her caregivers about baptism and church membership. It is best to allow the person time to understand baptism and church membership before she makes the decision to be baptized.

Arrange for the person to talk with the pastor about the actual procedures of baptism. Show him the inside of the empty baptistry and explain how high the water will be when he is in it. Assure him the pastor will be waiting in the baptistry for him and will remain there the entire time.

Baptism for the Person Who Uses a Wheelchair

What about the person who uses a wheelchair? Persons use wheelchairs for many reasons. The decision to baptize and how to do it takes in many considerations—the nature of the physical disability, the degree of mobility, how the person accepts additional supports. The best approach to this is a team decision. Include the wishes and advice of the person, a family member or caregiver, any professional such as a physical therapist or doctor, the pastor. In cases where the person can be baptized, some churches:

- provide manpower to help the person into the baptistry and support her during the baptism.
- arrange to hold the baptism at an indoor aquatics center equipped with body lifts to help get physically disabled persons in and out of the water.
- conduct the baptism in the shallow end of a pond.

If full traditional baptism is truly risky for the person, yet she desires to be obedient to Christ's command, talk with the pastor about creative ways to observe the ordinance that will still focus on the meaning of baptism. Any creative approaches to baptism should be performed in front of as many of the church body as possible, with the same degree of worship and ritual as a traditional baptism.

Baptism for the Person Who Is Afraid of the Water

What if the person to be baptized is afraid of the water? The first and obvious response is not to push baptism. Wait, observe, and let there be spiritual growth. Accept the person where she is. Talk with parents and caregivers. It may be a matter of the person learning simple water-safety skills such as floating in the shallow end of the swimming pool. Or perhaps your pastor can suggest a way to baptize that person without completely covering her face with water. If the person is insistent about being baptized, find a way to help her overcome her fears. If her fear of water holds her back from being baptized, assure her God understands her fears and that her decision to accept Christ will not be thwarted.

Church Membership

Encourage members of your church who have mental disabilities to enjoy the same privileges as other members.

Giving money.—He feels a sense of pride when he helps to support the work of the church. Even though he only had a quarter to put in the offering, Rob faithfully brought his money to the Lord each week. He did it with a smile because he loved giving to the church.

Praying.—Genuine care and sensitivity is expressed in the prayers of my mentally disabled friends like no other prayers I've heard. When our class prayed for the preacher, they really talked to God on his behalf. They loved and appreciated their pastor and truly believed God would care for him.

Supporting missions.—Persons with mental disabilities should be involved in local missions, learn about international missions and peoples groups, and encourage North American missionaries. The woman was mentally handicapped and abused. She had lived as a bag lady until the staff at the mission center ministered to her. Because of their caring she did volunteer work at the Baptist inner city mission center. She often witnessed to the people who came in for help. She could share firsthand about her experiences. She shared about experiences the missionaries could never know about or understand, but the people with whom she shared easily identified with her.

Voting in business meetings.—The mentally handicapped adult is often capable of understanding both sides of an issue when it is explained in words he understands. He can form his own conclusion. I was surprised when one of my class members voted *no* to accepting a friend as a candidate for church membership.

"Why?" I asked.

"Because I've known her a long time. I never believe what she says." It was an honest conviction.

Growing spiritually.—Involve the mentally disabled member in Discipleship Training and other programs that help her develop a closer relationship with God.

Adapt Discipleship Training materials for a class of mentally disabled adults.

Assign prayer partners in Sunday School and teach members how to pray with each other at church and throughout the week.

Help members apply biblical principles to their lives.

Witnessing to others.—Teach persons with mental disabilities how to tell others about Jesus. Tell the person with a mental disability to follow these steps.

• Pray and ask the Holy Spirit's direction.
• Make friends with people you meet.
• Be helpful and kind.
• As the friendship develops, listen for the times you can tell what God does for you.

- Invite new friends to church.
- Invite prospects to church parties, to listen to your favorite Christian CD or cassette tape, to see your new witness-wear shirt.
- Don't try to push your friends to believe in Jesus. When they ask, tell them how they can be friends with God. (The nonverbal member can do this on her communication device or with sign language.)
- Pray that your friend will accept Jesus as Savior.

Explain to persons with mental disabilities that lifestyle is most effective when witnessing to friends and family. Parents see the difference in the life of their adult daughter since she started attending Sunday morning Bible study. Trainers at the workplace notice that members of a certain Sunday School class are more helpful and cooperative at work. A house manager notices subtle changes in residents' behaviors since they have been attending a weekly Bible study.

Church membership also means the opportunity to worship and fellowship with other believers.

[1]From the Holy Bible, *New International Version*, copyright © 1973, 1978, 1984 by International Bible Society. Subsequent quotations are marked NIV.

How to Become a Christian

God loves you. That is the most important truth you can learn. The Bible says: "For God loved the world so much that he gave his only Son, so that everyone who believes in him may not die but have eternal life" (John 3:16, GNB).[1]

Even though you have done things that are not pleasing to God, He loves you. He loves you very much. He sent Jesus, His Son, to earth. Jesus showed us what God is like. Jesus lived, died, and was raised to live again.

Here is how to believe in Jesus: Know for sure that Jesus died and was raised back to life for you. Tell God that you have done wrong things. Ask God to forgive you. Promise not to do the wrong things anymore. Ask Jesus to be Lord of your life.

After you believe in Jesus, do the things Jesus would want you to do. Jesus would want you to obey the teachings of the Bible. That includes: (1) love God; (2) worship God; (3) pray to God; and (4) love other people.

People who believe in Jesus are called *Christians*. You can become a Christian today by doing the things you have read. If you ask Jesus to be your Savior and Lord, or if you would like to know more about becoming a Christian, talk to your Sunday School teacher, parents, pastor, or a Christian friend.

Remember, God loves you! Would you like to become a Christian?

[1]This quotation is from the *Good News Bible*, the Bible in Today's English Version. Old Testament: Copyright © American Bible Society 1976; New Testament: Copyright © American Bible Society 1966, 1971, 1976. Used by permission.

Q&A

What are the five *A's* of sharing God's love?

1. _____

2. _____

3. _____

4. _____

5. _____

One of your class members who uses a wheelchair desires to be baptized. How would you approach any dilemma this may cause?

_____

_____

_____

1. How much does God love the world?
2. What is sin? Who sins?
3. Why did God send Jesus?
4. Do we need to choose to believe in Jesus or not?
5. Do we need to tell God about our choice to believe?
6. Are we to tell others about our new belief?

Congratulations! You are now ready to tell a person with mental disabilities how to become a Christian. Pray that the Holy Spirit will direct you to someone this week so you can share your faith.

Respond to this statement: Persons with mental disabilities do not need to be saved. They are safe because they have not reached a mental age of accountability.

_____

_____

_____

A Place for Worshiping

A place for worshiping:
• encourages a daily quiet time.
• leads in thanksgiving and praise.
• models intercessory prayer.
• allows for participation in public worship.
plans for those who cannot attend corporate worship.

They held their hands high and signed enthusiastically while we sang. The deaf section was in the first few rows on the left-hand side of the worship center.

It was a night of firsts: my first time at Glorieta Conference Center;[1] the opening worship service; the first time I saw two dozen or more people who were deaf signing hymns together. In the New Mexico altitude, I had a difficult time breathing and singing at the same time, so I watched the signers. I thought of Psalm 63:4, "I will praise you as long as I live, and in your name I will lift up my hands" (NIV).2

That was it—holy hands lifted in praise to God. I couldn't believe the sense of worship it pictured! Worship—telling God how great He is. Many people of all types from several states were coming together to worship God.

We worship God individually and as a corporate body with actions that express our love and adoration for Him. God seeks worship. He reveals His desire for worship in Scriptures. The activities of a public worship service should be the reflections of the individual's daily worship of God.

God desires all people worship Him, no matter the degree of their disabilities. God can enable all of nature to sing praises to His name. We can be assured that He is able to bring praise to Himself, even from the person with severe multiple disabilities.

A place for everyone is a place where sincere devotion is expressed in prayer, music, confession, and Bible study. It is a place that welcomes everyone to worship God publicly.

Encourage Worship

Martha knows how to worship. She uses her musical talents to sing her praises to God and to lead others in worship. She talks sincerely to God about everything in her life. She doesn't attempt to sugarcoat her sins, either. She confesses them and asks God to enable her to live in ways that please Him. Martha tells me she would rather deal with sins quickly and get it over with. She prays: "Lord, help me learn my lesson from this situation as quickly as possible. I don't want anything to get in the way of my fellowship with You." You might think that such a friend would be dull and other-worldly. Not so! She is one of the wittiest and most fun-to-be with people I know. Her life flows naturally with thanksgiving and praises for the things God does and is. With a friend like her, I am encouraged to learn about the true value of worship and the joy and delight that come from worshiping God each day.

A church for everyone looks for every opportunity to win lost persons to Jesus Christ and to include those persons in worship. As a Sunday School teacher or a church leader, you are in a prime position to help persons with disabilities learn about the true value of worship and the joy and delight of worshiping God individually and publicly. You are also in a position to help your church body look for opportunities where persons with disabilities might lead in worship.

Encourage Daily Quiet Time

We can express our adoration and love for God in many ways. This means all people can worship. Psalm 8:2 tells us, "From the lips of children and infants, you have ordained praise" (NIV). Remind members with disabilities that God gives each of us the ability to worship Him.

Witness to the truth that God meets needs and gives guidance through a daily quiet time. A time of communication with God involves Bible study, prayer, and other forms of worship.

Encourage your members to read and study the Bible by recommending printed materials and guides that can help them develop self-discipline and continuity in their study time. These can be read-through-the-Bible guides or topical studies. If some of these members cannot read, recommend audiocassette recordings of Scripture or simple Bible stories they can listen to each day. Be certain the content of any material you recommend is biblically sound.

Encourage them to learn Scripture. If they are mentally handicapped, help them to learn simple Bible truths or to memorize one Bible verse each month. To promote the learning have contests, keep a chart, or provide posters members can hang in their rooms at home. All teachers, regardless of the class, can develop many creative ways to help members learn and remember Scripture.

Be alert to suggestions that encourage the members with disabilities in their daily prayer time. The person who is blind may tape record his prayer list. The nonverbal member can use her communication board or devise. The person with physical disabilities can rely on the strength and power available in prayer to accomplish things she's not able to do physically. The person with learning disabilities will find worth and acceptance in his daily conversations with God.

Encourage members with disabilities to use music in daily quiet time. Music is an expression that delights God, and it can help them worship at all times of the day. Hum a praise at work or school; listen to recordings in the car or to fall asleep at night. Sing Scripture back to God as a form of prayer. The only requirement is that they make a joyful noise, not a beautiful note. And if they can't sing or speak, they can express rhythm and poetry with sign language. Music helps them remember spiritual truths. The combination of rhythm and words in hymns and praises makes it much easier to remember the reasons why they worship God.

To paraphrase an old hymn, the cares of this world pale and dim in the light of God's favor and magnificence. Encourage your members with disabilities to thank God and praise God each time they worship. "How good it is to sing praises to our God, how pleasant and fitting to praise Him" (Ps. 147:1, NIV). Thanksgiving and praise exalt God for the qualities that make Him different from us—His purity and holiness, His goodness. Nothing in this world can compare to the characteristics God reveals about Himself. Thanks and praise help put life into a different perspective and cast aside deficiencies, disappointments, frustrations, and concerns.

A prayer partnership is an excellent way for members with disabilities to extend the vision of worship and to take part in intercessory prayer. Praying with other members in the class or church builds a unique type of intimacy. Partnerships might be arranged among members of the same Sunday School department or formed across age and ability lines. Most adults with mental disabilities will have prayer partners from their own Sunday School department. However, nothing prevents integration between their department and another group of adults.

God eliminates the disability status when He works through the prayers of His people. Encourage nondisabled members to seek prayer partners with disabled members and experience unique blessings.

Encourage Public Worship

Consider these examples.

The stroke Marge experienced while in her early twenties weakened her left leg and twisted the right side of her face. Surprisingly, her skills at the piano and organ were not impaired. She was a good musician, but it was difficult for her to climb two steps to the organ on the pulpit platform. Church members solved that problem by moving the organ to a ground-level platform addition.

Before his vision became greatly impaired, Carl often read Scripture and gave announcements because he has a beautiful speaker's voice. Members of the congregation did not want to lose the quality Carl voice brings to their worship. With the help of large-print materials and magnification aids, Carl is still able to lead in the worship service.

How does your church involve persons with disabilities in worship? Is the soloist who uses a wheelchair invited to share her talents? Is the man with cerebral palsy invited to pray aloud? Is your Sunday School director blind or hearing impaired?

Many persons with disabilities think they are not welcomed in places of public worship. Highly intelligent, professional persons with disabilities have told me the church looks down on them, doesn't want them, and judges them because they are disabled. These people truly believe all churches feel that way about them. What message does your church send to persons with disabilities? How can you encourage them to worship with you?

Accessibility is a good place to begin welcoming persons with disabilities to your worship center.

- Provide wheelchair accessibility to the choir loft.
- Place hearing amplification in various locations throughout the worship center.
- Shorten three or more pews or rows to make room for a wheelchair at the end and at various locations throughout the worship center.
- Position persons who are deaf so they can see both the interpreter and the speaker at the same time.
- Make certain the lighting in that area is adequate and without glare.

The families of persons with mental disabilities want them to participate in worship. It will help if these persons know what to expect and how to behave appropriately. Sunday School teachers can teach about the different parts of the worship service and how members are expected to behave. Other church members can volunteer to sit with individuals and model appropriate behavior for them.

Churches can also provide options for the person who cannot attend an entire service.

- *Extended session.*—Teachers design their own order of worship with singing, prayer, and the Bible truths learned in Sunday School. They also plan craft activities and refreshments.

- *Surrogate grandparents*.—Older couples sit with the child with mental disabilities in the worship center until the preaching begins; then they take the child outside for recreation and a Bible story. Parents are free to worship without worry or stress.

- *One-on-one.*—Church members provide care on a rotation basis for a young teen who has unpredictable behavior outbursts. A speaker system and one-way glass wall installed in a room directly behind the worship center allow the worker and teen to take part in the service without disturbing others.

Is your church a place of worship for everyone? Do persons with disabilities feel welcomed to your Bible studies and worship services?

Hattie tells about a neighbor she had when she lived in Brazil. This 12- or 13-year-old boy knew to show up at their house every evening at the dinner hour. This missionary family was willing to feed him. Of course he had to sit through their prayer time and family worship, but that was agreeable with him. He couldn't talk, so all he had to do was listen. But he enjoyed what he heard about a God who loved him through this family. He listened more intently each time he came for dinner. Then one night, he wanted to be included. He gestured and gluttered his desires so that Hattie could understand. He wanted to pray to this loving God. "So we let him. And he did talk to God, only we couldn't understand much of what he

was trying to say. But you know, I firmly believe that God did and that this boy got through to the throne with his worship."

[1]For more information about Glorieta Conference Center, call 1-800-797-4222; FAX, (505) 757-6149; or write, Glorieta Conference Center, Reservations Department, P.O. Box 8, Glorieta, NM 87535.

[2]From the Holy Bible, *New International Version*, copyright © 1973, 1978, 1984 by International Bible Society. Subsequent quotations are marked NIV.

Q&A

What about persons who cannot read? How can they have a daily worship time? List your suggestions:

- _____

- _____

- _____

- _____

If you were responsible for helping a person with mental disabilities be aware of the value of corporate worship, what steps would you take?

_____

_____

_____

_____

_____

_____

_____

_____

_____

Practice the signs for these words. Write a brief prayer using as many of them as possible. Pray and use sign language as you worship.

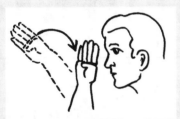

LOVE
S-hands cross on heart.

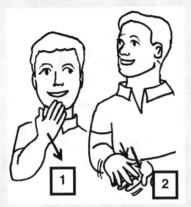

PRAISE
Flat hand on chin, then clap hands.

WORSHIP
Left hand closed over right, move toward body in slight verticle circle.

Illustrations used by permission from *Signing Exact English,* © 1980 Modern Signs Press, Inc.

GOD
Palm-left B arcs down from above to near forehead.

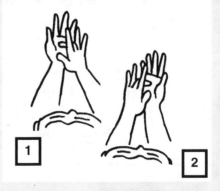

JESUS
Bent right middle finger touches left palm, reverse. (Nails in the hands of Jesus)

HOLY
Right H circles above left palm, then flat hand wipes off palm.

SPIRIT
9-hand's palms-facing, separate up and down in wavy motion.

A Place for Fellowshiping

A place for fellowship:
• includes fellowship with individuals.
• focuses on fellowship in the Sunday School class and department.
• involves fellowship with other departments and other churches.

Sam chose to sit across the table from Gloria and Lars. I watched as he kept them entertained throughout the meal. They seemed to think he was delightfully witty.

The young couple talked with Sam as if they had known him for years, which was not the case, since they had only met him that day. Considering that Sam is nonverbal and can communicate only with gestures and sounds, all that conversation could seem like quite a feat. Those of us who are familiar with Sam know that being nonverbal doesn't often stop Sam from making his thoughts known, nor does it keep him from making friends quickly.

This was our regularly scheduled fellowship. One Sunday each month, we invited another Adult Sunday School department to have lunch with our special education department. We arranged for the different departments to mix and mingle at the tables. That way, other adults had the opportunity to get acquainted with our adults with mental disabilities.

The response was always positive. Gloria told me meeting Sam truly changed her perspective about people with multiple disabilities.

Fellowship is one of the primary reasons people go to church. Fellowship implies the community we have with others in our church. It is friendship and comradeship. There is a sense of equality, of being on the same level among those who fellowship together.

Fellow church members and fellow believers like to meet together for friendship, fun, recreation, or leisure activities. This type of fellowship gives us opportunity to know one another, share our joys and sorrows, and build trust. Actually there is nothing quite like sincere fellowship of one believer with another believer.

Fellowship does not just occur or materialize on its own. In today's busy world, we have to plan and schedule times for fellowship.

Most people find their initial church friends and fellowship through the Sunday School. All Sunday School departments that have a member with disabilities need to take extra care to see that she is included in all fellowship opportunities. Teachers and class members need to make an effort to build relationships with her both inside and outside the church setting.

A place for fellowshiping is the place where we can get to know and be friends with people who share our love for Jesus Christ.

Fellowship with Individuals

I had two different Sunday School teachers named Norma. One was my teacher when I was a young teen; the other was my teacher when my children were small. These were two milestones in my life. Both Normas made an effort to spend time with me as an individual outside of church. Because of that effort, both rank highly as two of the most effective teachers and spiritual leaders I've known. Their examples have served me well in my role as a Sunday School leader.

Why? Both Normas were able to teach me the Bible because they took time to know me. They were able to help me realize the importance of applying biblical principles to my questions and needs. As a Sunday School worker, I realize a little time spent knowing my members as individuals goes a long way in being able to teach them about God.

Simple? In theory. It isn't always easy to be involved in individual lives. But it is always important enough to make the effort. In the department for adults with mental disabilities, fellowship is an unparalleled support of Bible study in impacting others' lives with spiritual truths.

Persons with mental disabilities want you to know them. They want to tell you about the foods they like, the latest movie they saw, their boyfriends and girlfriends, happenings at work and school. They, more than any group of people you may ever teach, desire your interest in the everyday things of their lives. Your members with disabilities need to believe you are truly concerned about the things that concern them and that you genuinely love them enough to listen, remember, teach, and even correct when necessary. When you get to know each of them, you begin to understand more about the nature of people, the grace of God, the fact that persons with mental disabilities are a great deal like yourself.

The adult with mental disabilities who comes to your class or department may have a personal history foreign to most adults you know. She may have spent many of her formative years in an institution or in a large-capacity group home. She currently may live in a home with eight other adults. She may never have had a bedroom to herself. She possibly knows little about true privacy or personal ownership. Her life always may have been dictated by someone else. She is going to perceive life differently from you. Everyday examples with a spiritual twist, such as a loving father or a heavenly home, may not mean the same things to her. To be a more effective teacher, you need to be aware of her background. How do you learn about it? Get to know her away from church.

The mentally disabled person in your class may live with his family, be involved in school, a day program or a work center, play on sports teams, have special hobbies and interests. In order to help him apply biblical truths to his life, you need to know his family members, the names of his teachers or work supervisors, facts about his sports team. Applying Bible truths to his life means knowing what his life is about.

The prime way to know a person is to spend time with that person, one-on-one, talking and getting acquainted. The best way to convince a person with mental disabilities that God desires a personal relationship with us, wants us to talk with Him, and listen to His Word is to give her positive reference points about relationships in her own life.

How can you do that with your members? Customize these suggestions to your teaching situation.

Go to their homes.—Schedule a time to go where each member lives. Explain, "I've just come to say hello and to meet family members or residential staff." Learn the names of the people your members live with. Get acquainted with family and friends and let them see you are genuinely interested in your class member. When several of your members live in the same facility, give equal attention to each one. Ask to see Marv's flower garden, Heather's newest painting, Lannie's new TV.

Go to where they work.—Learn the names of case managers or service coordinators. They want to know that you are a proactive advocate and friend. Work center staff members want to show you their facilities and introduce you to the services they provide. Your members will be honored and delighted you came to see them at work. If several of your members work at the same center, plan a time when you can eat lunch with them in the cafeteria. If you have never done this before, you are in for a true experience. You will get to meet boyfriends and girlfriends, watch how social dynamics are carried out, make new friends, and discover or reach prospects for your class.

Go to the school.—Make arrangements to visit your member's class at a time when he can show you around or when he can see you there. Attend special programs. Praise your member for his school accomplishments. One teacher shares: "I didn't know one thing about multiple disabilities when I agreed to help in that Sunday School class. But I did know many of those kids went to a class at our area high school for persons with severe multiple disabilities. So I asked one of the mothers to introduce me to the teacher. I obtained permission to visit and observe some of the things the kids were learning. Soon I was volunteering three hours a week as a lunch-time helper. I know that the kids now recognize me, and I've learned so many things about how to teach them at church. I recommend visiting the schools."

Go for a treat.—Is it possible for you to take each member for a snack? Maybe you could try to go twice each year? If it is possible, please try to do it. It doesn't need to be a fancy or costly place. An ice cream parlor or drive-through window at a hamburger restaurant is ideal. (Keep dietary restrictions in mind!) Many adults with mental disabilities don't get to have this type of outing often, so the personal attention is special to them. You probably won't need to encourage your member to talk about herself. She will!

Give a call.—A five-minute phone call each week remains the best way to get acquainted with any class member. Ask a simple question, "How was your day?" Keep notes on what members share with you so you can remember what is going on in their lives.

Write a note.—Even members who cannot read like to receive mail. Send postcards with bright pictures and a simple message.

Fellowship in the Class

A small department or a study group allows members the opportunity to fellowship with one another at church. This is one of its advantages. Consider how these key points in the class setting enhance the fellowship among members.

Before the session begins.—In many churches, members come to church on the van, arriving at church as much as 20 to 30 minutes before time for Sunday School to start. Experienced teachers know it is imperative that a teacher be in the room when these members arrive and that this early half-hour be included in the teaching schedule. While some classes provide activities for early arrivers, others structure an informal chat session.

This allows members the time to tell about the important things that happened to them during the week. One teacher explained: "They're going to talk about these things anyway. My members know this is the time we talk about personal bits and pieces of information. Then it is out of the way and doesn't interfere with the teaching time as much." This fellowship time lets members learn the skill of listening which is fundamental to true friendships.

We could always count on Carie to be ready with some sort of news on Sunday mornings. "Jim isn't my boyfriend anymore; I'm going to start a new job next week; Trish got into trouble with the house manager this morning." Somehow her type of news started conversation. We learned about what had been going on in our members' lives. It certainly helped us know how to help members apply biblical principles to the real things in their lives that week.

Some classes serve snacks when members first arrive. If you do provide food at anytime during Sunday School, plan for fruit juice and low-sugar foods. Avoid caffeine products, soft drinks, doughnuts. Again, watch members' dietary needs.

Prayer time.—Practical fellowship occurs when members pray with one another every Sunday. Members will be ready with prayer requests each week if they know you are going to ask for them. This helps members learn to articulate their concerns and desires to one another and to God. Requests may be as simple as: "My Mommy"; "I can get a new job"; or as thoughtful as: "Pray for my friend's family. Her brother was hurt in a bad car accident."

The art of fellowship is developed when teachers ask members to pray for one another's concerns: "Paula, please thank God for Ryan's mother." "Jason, will you ask God to lead David to the right job." "Michelle, please pray for Susan's friends." "Patty, ask God to help the brother who has been hurt."

Teaching time.—For the member with lower-skills abilities, fellowship can be as basic as learning to share materials, time, space, and the teacher's attention with

other members. Each step in the learning environment allows opportunities for members to develop skills of self-expression and to gain feelings of acceptance. They also learn appropriate basic social skills—how to greet a fellow class member, how to encourage others with a smile, how to take part in group activities. By taking their cues from teachers' behaviors, they learn how to laugh, tease, joke, and have a good time enjoying one another's company.

Fellowship and a sense of community are built when teachers plan activities and learning situations appropriate for members' ages and skills abilities. Such planning pulls the small group or class together and says to each member, "This is the place where you belong, where you fit with the rest of the group."

Fellowship as a Department

All Sunday School departments for adults with mental disabilities need to have regularly scheduled social events for members and prospects. What you can do at these events and how many you have each year may depend on the services offered by other agencies and churches in your area.

Professionals began over 30 years ago to look at ways to deinstitutionalize social services for mentally retarded youth and adults. They quickly identified a common factor about that population—lack of leisure time opportunities. There were simply no places for them to go to have fun. Many adults lived at home without the services of day programs and work centers. Social lives centered around upper-age parents. In addition, few churches had Special Education Sunday School classes. By identifying this need, advocates did a great service for persons with mental disabilities. Agencies and churches quickly responded by providing the missing services and ministries.

Perhaps you live where churches sponsor all the social events for mentally disabled adults in your county. Experienced teachers have developed many creative ways to do this on a weekly or monthly basis. No matter which state they live in, when teachers share with me about these events, they seem to do one thing in common. They capitalize on nature and its resources. They try to do as many outdoor activities as possible when weather permits. They go:

- to the beach or a swimming pool.
- to zoos or nature reserves.
- to mountain retreats.
- on nature hikes and exercise trails.
- on overnight camping trips.

I've heard fascinating stories about bonfires on the beaches in Florida, day-trips to the mountains in all places that have mountains nearby, and sandpit volleyball on the plains— all done by groups of mentally disabled adults and sponsors. Because this is such an encompassing ministry, churches involve the talents of the many people in the community who are willing to help with these large projects.

"Our community doesn't have a local chapter of Arc, and our work center is small. Between our town and neighboring ones we may have 150 adults with mental disabilities served by eight churches. Teachers from each of the churches plan all the social events for the members. That helps the house managers, and we feel like that makes our efforts a true ministry to many people. Since we are small communities, many of our friends and neighbors are willing to help us plan and sponsor events," explained one worker.

In places where Arc, residential centers, and work programs provide more than enough opportunities for social outings, creative church workers:

- plan quarterly fellowships.
- cooperate with other agencies to help sponsor events.
- make certain that church events are scheduled on the community calendar.
- plan annual retreats for the county or entire state.

"We held a one-day retreat at our local Baptist association's campground. It was mid-October, and I think God gave us a perfectly pristine day just for Charlie. We planned most of the activities outdoors with the blue of the lake as our background, enhancing everything we did. Charlie lived in an intermediate care facility about five miles from the camp. He didn't get out much, and the day in a country setting meant so much to him. He cried when the day was over because he had never before spent such a wonderful day outside," a teacher said.

Teachers share extensive lists of ideas for social events and fellowships. These suggestions can spark ideas as you plan for your members.

- Vocal music groups or handbell choirs
- Performance and drama groups
- Annual spring or Christmas banquets
- Craft classes
- Cooking and woodworking classes
- Lunch once a month at a local cafeteria or after church in the fellowship hall
- Fishing trips
- Bowling leagues
- Skating or skiing parties
- Professional sports events
- Pizza parties
- Board games at the church each Friday night
- Movie night at the church
- Fall Festival and Valentine's Day parties
- Monthly birthday celebrations
- Super Bowl parties
- Tours and out-of-town trips
- Track and field events

Many churches plan some of these social events to include parents, caregivers, and siblings. Your members' parents are an appreciative support group for your ministry. Get to know them when at all possible. Chat about friendly things such as their hobbies and interests. Go to lunch with a mother, or get a parents-only support group together for an evening of fellowship.

If you have several teachers in your department, plan fellowships for teachers.

- Have miniretreats for planning and prayer.
- Eat dinner after church with all teachers and their families.
- Sponsor teacher appreciation banquets.
- Bake the teacher's favorite cake or casserole for his or her birthday.

Most social events require that you plan ahead. Get all details squared away: location; reservations, if necessary; date and time; number of workers and sponsors needed; food arrangements; and cost per person.

Announce your plans early, so members will reserve the date and have time to invite their friends. Have a publicity piece or brochure to send home to caregivers, parents, or apartment trainers.

Include a registration form. Do have a deadline for registration forms and fees; it helps participants as well as workers. Some teachers encourage participants to

register early by giving a price break for early registration.

Provide a schedule for events lasting over two hours. Participants and caregivers want to know what they can expect.

Prepare a social calendar each month of the year. Print a calendar grid on one side of an 8 1/2-by-11 inch sheet of paper. Type in the social events and important dates and make a copy for each member. This project can be the responsibility of your Sunday School department's social committee, an excellent ministry for members with higher skills abilities.

For all-day and overnight events, you must have an emergency medical authorization signed by a parent or guardian. Do not allow any participant to attend the event without a signed authorization. Keep that authorization in your possession while at the event.

Be informed about persons who need to take medication during all-day and overnight events. Your state will have a set of guidelines or regulations concerning the dispensing of medication in such cases. In some cases, it may be necessary for a residential staff person to attend.

Know what type of driver's license your state requires for the driver of large-capacity vans; follow insurance regulations.

If you hold camps and other extended events, include a nurse as a staff worker. Be certain the nurse is aware of fragile medical conditions among participants. Always have a medical emergency plan for any type of event.

Fellowship with Other Departments

Other church members are interested in knowing your members and may be curious about proper ways they can interact. Many churches testify to the benefits of planned social events that integrate members of the special education department with other departments or church groups. In addition to involving other groups in the previous suggestions, departments for adults with mental disabilities can:
- host an open house each month and invite one department to study the Bible with them.
- visit children's and preschool classes with a biblical skit and songs.
- make Christmas craft projects for each adult department.
- provide entertainment at a senior citizen luncheon.
- share prayer requests with other groups.
- form secret pals with adults from other departments.

"We plan at least one social event each month which integrates our department with at least one other church group. Our members participate in many of the churchwide fellowship functions. If an event is open to the body of our church, it is open to us," explained a special education teacher.

Fellowship with Other Churches

"One of the churches in our local Baptist association volunteers each year to host our spring special education banquet. It is an outreach event sponsored by our Baptist association for all adults in our community who have mental disabilities. All churches with special education departments are encouraged to attend and bring prospects. The host church's youth group serves and cleans up after the event. Our adults respond warmly to the teens who, in turn, respond warmly to them. The senior pastor and the youth minister are there to help clean dirty tables and dishes. Their presence affirms each teacher and member."

We often hear there is strength in numbers. The saying certainly seems true when it comes to ministry. We learned many years ago that what one church in our Baptist association cannot accomplish for persons with mental disabilities, several churches working together can accomplish successfully and with less effort.

Churches in the same community or Baptist association, working together for persons with mental disabilities, help to strengthen community ties. Their combined efforts say a great deal to the community about Christlike love, commitment, and sincere concern for all people.

Churches find that cooperation on many events, especially social events, multiplies the outreach potential for any one church. In some cases, churches plan large events for the entire Baptist association. Other times, groups of two or three churches will plan to do something together. Either way, the work for the good of the community becomes ours instead of yours and mine.

Cooperation brings together not only the churches in the Baptist association, but also other agencies and churches of other denominations. The results are remarkably noticeable. It is a matter of influencing our communities for Jesus Christ, one changed life at a time.

One special education Bible study class combines the efforts of many churches in the same small community. The class is held in the building with the most accommodating space. Workers from each of the churches teach on a rotation schedule. Teachers meet monthly for an extensive planning period to assign responsibilities and develop strategies which results in continuity in the learning environment.

Q&A

List three reasons why it is helpful to know each of your department members personally.

- _____
- _____
- _____

Read about the ways to spend time with individual members. Is there one you haven't tried? How can you implement that suggestion with your members?

Respond to this statement: A small department or study group allows members opportunity to fellowship at church.

Think of one way your Sunday School department can fellowship with another department or church. Write your idea in this space.

_____

Look at your fellowship ideas. What types of preparations need to be made? Write a checklist.

A Place for Organizing

A Place for organizing:
- **provides room and supplies.**
- **plans for teacher development.**
- **helps with behavior management.**

One special education teacher has the following testimony. "When my husband took a pastorate here, I told him I would like to continue my ministry to adults with mental disabilities. I checked with another church in our small town where most of the adults with mental retardation went to Sunday School. The pastor of that church practically said that these people were not welcome; he didn't want them in his church. That really hurt me. I knew these people needed a place to study the Bible. Other members in our church committed to help me, but we didn't know where to put another class. We are truly a small church. There

was not one extra room available. One of the deacons remembered the small house at the back of the church property. The church used it for storage. A work team agreed to build a shed and clean out the old house. You should have seen it before we painted and cleaned. It was a mess! The work team built a ramp to the outside door on the kitchen side. That door was extra wide, and we could get wheelchairs through it. They also made the bathroom accessible for persons with physical disabilities. After that, there wasn't much money for equipment other than tables and chairs we gleaned from other departments. We were cramped for space in those days, but we thought of creative ways to stretch what we had."

Organizing your space, resources, and materials allows for maximum teaching efficiency in your special education department. Recording and keeping current information files about your members is also important.

If you are a first-time teacher in a special education department, starting the first-ever ministry for persons in your church who have mental disabilities, these answers should help you get a handle on the basic logistics.

You may have many years of experience as a teacher in a special education department with the best of resources, space, and a sufficient number of trained teachers. Look for new suggestions or insights. Realize many teachers in special education departments do not have your expertise or resources. This chapter may challenge you to search for a new teacher in your local area or state. Offer to share your knowledge, extra materials, and other resources. Help the new teacher solve problems she currently is facing in establishing her department.

Organization may not be an easy thing for you. Maybe the mere mention of the word makes you feel uncomfortable or even a bit intimidated. Do not be overwhelmed with the tasks of getting organized. The following ideas can help make your class learning environment inviting and safe.

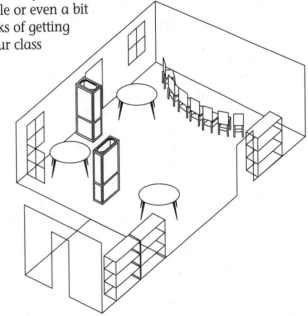

How big should our classroom be?

How should we arrange our room?

What suggestions are there for getting my room together?

Persons who are disabled need to have provisions equal to any other group in the church. They are entitled to it. That means, first of all, that your department and class rooms should have adequate lighting and ventilation and heating and cooling systems. Walls should be smooth, and at least one large wall should be suitable for displays. As with all Sunday School rooms, it needs adequate storage areas such as cupboards, cabinets, and a coat closet. In addition, rooms for persons with mental disabilities should be at ground level with rest rooms nearby. Both the rooms and rest rooms should be wheelchair accessible.

Ideally, the room should provide 25 square feet per person at 80 percent of the enrollment. The minimum room size for your department should be 20 feet wide and 24 feet long to accommodate basic furniture needs. Add 10 square feet per person for anticipated wheelchair needs. It is most important that you have adequate space for all members to sit and work comfortably. Avoid overcrowding for both learning and behavior reasons.

Provide sturdy folding chairs and provide enough tables to accommodate every four to six members. Round tables work best, but these are not always available.

A carpeted or non-skid floor is best. Never have throw rugs. Make certain all cracks in the linoleum or vinyl floors are repaired. Adults with mental disabilities often have visual and coordination problems. They stumble easily on poor walking surfaces.

It is best if you have areas for small-group activities, a large-group semicircle facing the display wall, and a quiet inviting corner or separate small room for a timeout center or for the individual who needs to be alone.

Our department rooms are far from ideal. There aren't even rest rooms nearby. What can we do?

I have endured all types of far-from-ideal classrooms for my special education groups. Our first class for adults with mental handicaps met in the overflow room where the church stored choir risers and the wedding ceremony paraphernalia. I determined the class would not meet in that room any longer than necessary. My strategy was based on education—informing the church staff about the needs of my members. Those were the days before the Americans with Disabilities Act (ADA) and communitywide building accessibility codes, both of which are advantageous tools for your current purposes.

Our area of the room had enough space for two long tables with chairs. At least the floor was carpeted nicely, and the walls were cleaned and smooth. I made certain our class area had sturdy tables and chairs. One of our deacon friends made a fantastic bulletin board for the focal wall. I could ignore the other things for a while. I concentrated on building the size of the group through personal visitation, by having well-prepared lessons, and by praying a lot. It didn't take long for the staff to notice how God was blessing us with visitors and new members. After we had the staff's attention, I talked with them about how we needed additional space and how choir risers and wedding gear were in the way. I talked about safety and liability issues involving persons with disabilities. It backfired! They moved our department to a basement classroom. We had plenty of space and storage all to ourselves, but the steps! And the rest rooms were even further away. But we continued to grow in numbers. The staff and the building committee sincerely wanted to bless the ministry with their support and did all they could to arrange good accommodations for us.

Talk with your church staff and Sunday School director about the type of space you need. They are interested in helping you. By all means talk about the rest room accommodations. Bladder control and other health-related problems are important issues for your members.

Until a more ideal space is available, make the most of what you have. You can make certain the walls are clean and painted in a light, neutral shade. If the floors are in poor condition, be creative about ways you get them fixed.

- Ask two or three adult classes to raise the funds for new flooring in your room.
- Talk to a local carpet and flooring dealer. You might be surprised at the generous donations one will make for a class like yours.
- Talk with the Church Council about plans to fix and improve the area. Be certain to stress the risks involved with poor floor surfaces.

Request good light fixtures and lighting. Ask for storage areas. Arrange your room so you can have small groups and a large-group area.

If you do not have a window in your room, ask an artist to paint an outdoor scene on a wall or display different posters for each season of the year. It does not take much money to make the room attractive and inviting.

Keep an inventory of basic supplies in your room:

- poster board
- white paper
- large sheets of paper in various colors
- construction paper
- felt-tip markers in various colors

- pens and pencils
- scissors
- tape and glue sticks
- an audiocassette tape recorder
- a department set of low-vocabulary Bibles

You may also choose to keep:

- Tempera™ paints
- colored chalk
- modeling clay

- paper towels
- dowel sticks
- rhythm instruments

We share a room with two other groups. We get it during Sunday School. The other groups use it on Sunday and Wednesday evenings. We are not allowed to put pictures on the walls, so there go our permanent displays. Each group has different furniture needs, and there is no storage area. What can we do to get the best use of our space?

Be convinced that, for Sunday School at least, the space in that room is for your members to use. Arrange tables and chairs for your time in the room. Three tables positioned near three corners can be small-group areas, and a semicircle near the center of the room can be the large-group area. If all your members meet as one large group, arrange tables in a *U* formation. Place the chairs so all members can see the focal wall.

Ask the building committee for a minimum of two combination chalk/bulletin boards to be placed on separate walls. That alone can make the room multipurpose. Or suggest that cork message bars (low-cost items available at office-supply stores) be positioned on every wall. They are easy to mount and have dozens of uses for displaying posters, pictures, charts—whatever you need to put on a wall. Display only what you need for that lesson and take it down at the end of the session.

Also request at least three wall-mounted cabinets with locks. Probably the other two groups would appreciate their own storage cabinet as much as you would. The fronts of cabinets are handy for displays. Be careful about using sticky putty and tape.

Alternative solutions for churches with low budgets include the following items.

- Stand a large three-sided display board on a table. You can buy one at most office and art-supply stores. Or you can easily make your own with cardboard, self-adhesive plastic, and vinyl tape.
- Display pictures on the back of a shelf unit, a piano, on window glass.
- Use a portable room divider/bulletin board.
- Construct a low-cost, four-sided unit. Cover one side with cork board, the other side with dry-erase material, the ends with peg board.
- Store writing and art supplies in a large fishing tackle box.
- Buy your own two-drawer filing cabinet for the room. Keep supplies locked in it when not in use. Cover the filing cabinet and use it as a table top.

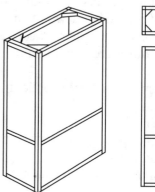

- If no storage is available at the church, store supplies in a heavy cardboard box, a poultry box, or plastic crate. Carry your supplies and materials to and from the room each week.

What do you mean by small-group time and large-group time? How do I group members?

Small-group time provides for a good learning environment. Teachers form small groups to help members understand spiritual truths at their levels of spiritual and cognitive abilities.

Small-group time works best with a teacher member ratio of 1:1 for the severely disabled member and 1:6 for members with higher skills abilities.

The teaching procedures in *Special Education Teacher Packet*[1] suggest members meet in small groups when they first arrive, so teachers can pique their interests for that session's study emphasis and to know when to help members apply biblical truth to their own lives.

The large-group time is when all groups come together for the Bible story, songs, prayer, and Bible verse.

Teachers generally find three distinct learning groups. The lower skills-abilities group includes persons who cannot read and who may be nonverbal. The higher skills-abilities group includes persons who read on a 3rd- to 5th-grade level with a certain degree of comprehension. The mid group has some reading or word recognition skills.

Where do I find workers?

Look for potential workers in every adult age group from college to senior adults. A simple questionnaire often helps you pinpoint the people in your church who are interested in working with your members.

- Don't neglect to invite the new church member to visit your class. Many teachers currently working in special education departments were introduced to the ministry within a few weeks of joining the church.
- Workers who help with one of the department's social events or special education VBS often feel impressed to teach in the Sunday School department because of the members' winsome openness and friendliness.
- Teachers who have "retired" after many years with the same age group are usually not satisfied sitting in a Sunday School class. They get excited about the opportunity to use their skills in creative ways with your members.

- A parent of a mentally disabled person can be a potential worker in your department. However, most of the time, the parent needs the support and nurturing of her own peer group, and she needs time away from her child. It is best if the parent/worker is a mature Christian with a good support group, works in the department after the child moves away from home or is deceased, and is not asked to work with his or her child.

Pray about the names of potential workers. Ask God for His leadership. Talk to other church leaders about how potential leaders have previously exhibited dependability and commitment to their responsibilities. Do not consider someone who is emotionally unstable or who has a reputation for not following through on his or her commitment.

Contact each person you feel strongly impressed to approach.

1. Tell her why you feel she would make a good teacher in your department.

2. Ask her to visit your department for one session or to let you show and explain teaching materials and members' magazines.

3. Ask her to pray about the matter. Agree on a date when you will contact her again about her decision.

4. Never pressure a potential teacher into accepting the position.

Qualifications and characteristics for special education workers are to:

- love God.
- be active, growing Christians.
- be an enthusiastic and lifelong learner.
- live a moral lifestyle.
- be a church member and loyal to the church.
- display a call from God to teach persons who are mentally disabled.
- have a love for persons who have mental retardation; enjoy being around them.
- be able to cope physically and emotionally with the demands of teaching.
- understand the development and learning characteristics of persons with mental disabilities.
- be responsive to the many forms of communication used by members.
- be willing to visit.
- be willing to plan.
- be committed to studying, preparing, and using the resources in effective teaching.
- be cooperative.
- be fun-loving.
- be confident, but accepting of personal limitations.
- be creative, flexible, friendly, patient, kind, and understanding.
- enable members to do for themselves.
- be firm, but gentle.
- have concern for families and caregivers.

What draws workers to the special education department?

Many reasons draw workers to the special education department.

Bite-size pieces.—Potential workers are more likely to accept a specific responsibility—a job that seems "doable" for a set amount of time, within a certain time frame, rather than a list of duties that appear burdensome and overwhelming.

Wording in your request.—"Would you be willing to lead a small-group activity each Sunday morning from 9:30 to 10:00?" is less threatening than, "We need a teacher for 25 adults during Sunday School."

Bible study.—Potential workers often agree to serve when they see the quality and focus of the Bible study materials. New teachers are impressed that we teach

the Bible to adults with mental handicaps at their level of understanding. New teachers are often surprised at the spiritual depth in each lesson.

A clear sense of purpose.—Many teachers testify, "Somehow I knew God wanted me to serve in the special education department."

Love for members.—Potential workers often discover they enjoy being with persons with mental disabilities and truly want God's best for them.

Mrs. G. retired after working in the Children's Division for more than 20 years. She tried going to her age-group class, but she realized she did not want to sit and listen. When I first approached her as a potential worker, she said she didn't think she could work with our members, but she would pray about it. I talked to her again in two weeks: "I remember how you faithfully telephoned the children every Saturday evening year after year. We could use a secretary to take attendance and call our members each week." Mrs. G. knew she could handle that. Within a few months she volunteered to lead the Bible verse activity each session. Not many weeks later, she was ready to teach a small group.

Where can teachers get training? Why are training sessions important?

Workers need to understand persons with mental disabilities and how to work with them. Training allows teachers to learn more about persons with mental disabilities. Training also allows teachers to discover their teaching strengths and gives ideas on how to increase effective teaching.

Training opportunities are offered through the local Baptist association and state Baptist convention offices. Summer conferences on special education are sponsored by the Baptist Sunday School Board at Glorieta Conference Center[2] and Ridgecrest Conference Center.[2] No matter how long you have taught or how new you are to the ministry, all teachers benefit from the insights and ideas of another person who works in this ministry. Each teacher should take part in training as often as possible.

How necessary are planning meetings?

Planning is essential. A weekly planning meeting is best, but if that is not possible for your teachers, try meeting once a month or once a quarter.

Experienced special education department workers say:

- planning improves communication among workers, provides for coordination, and links Special Education Sunday School to the work of the church.
- planning instills confidence.
- planning ahead gives you plenty of time to gather resources, photocopy handouts, and preenlist members who will help during the session.
- planning enables you to hear other people's ideas on what the Bible passage means and on how to conduct the teaching session.
- planning stops you from using the same teaching method week after week.
- planning prevents duplication.
- planning ensures at least one teacher is in the room before the first member arrives.
- planning guarantees that you set up the room and prepare activity areas before the session begins.
- planning keeps your session time focused on Bible truths.
- planning enables members to make choices among planned activities.
- planning keeps ministry, outreach, and evangelism as top priorities.
- planning reveals training needs and opportunities.

These five basic topics should be covered in regular department planning meetings:

Administration and training.—The department director should lead the discussion on enrollment goals and ways to accomplish them (See the "Special Education Sunday School Checkup" in the Appendix.), evaluate how well the department is meeting session goals, plan special activities, address training needs and opportunities, solve problems, and talk about the need for substitute or additional workers.

Reaching and witnessing.—The outreach-evangelism leader or secretary should lead the discussion on ways to reach prospects and enroll members, report about contacts made, update prospect files or database, tell visitation schedules, give attendance numbers, report about contacting absentees, and share about reaching inactive members.

Caring and fellowship.—Teachers should discuss specific needs of members and workers, plans for appropriate actions, plans for follow-up with new Christians, ways for workers to be included in members' activities, and plans for fellowship activities.

Teaching and learning.—The department director should lead discussions on what worked and what didn't work in the previous session and why, the Bible material for the next session, how any of the activities suggested in the teaching procedures should be adapted for individual members, the steps to be used in "Guide Bible Study," how much variety is being used in teaching methods, and gathering resources and supplies. Practicing specific activities to see how they work can cut down on problems on Sunday morning.

Praying.—The department director should lead teachers to share concerns for members, families/caregivers, prospects, the church, and one another. Seek God's guidance for the department.

What if there is only one worker in the special education department?

You are not alone. Other teachers in your church are planning a Sunday School session each week. Attend the regular planning meeting of teachers meeting; plan with other teachers. For instance, if children's workers use the *Life and Work Foundation Series*, you can review the Bible passage with them; plan with a teacher from another church; meet with members of your social committee to pray and plan fellowships. Do have a time each week when you prepare your teaching room and pray for your members.

It is important for each teacher to have a personal daily worship time. The most effective teachers are the ones who spend time alone with God each day. You can use the Bible reading schedule in the back of *Special Education Bible Study* or use *Open Windows*.[1] Concentrate your study on the Bible passage for the week or use another guide to help you study God's Word. Whichever you use, do it.

Are member information sheets really necessary?

Member information sheets are necessary. A sample of an information sheet is given in the Appendix. We encourage you to complete one for each member in your class or department. Consider printing the form on cardstock. Each 8 1/2 X 11 inch sheet should hold two forms. Separate the forms to make durable information cards suitable for filing. If your church develops a Person/Family-Centered Plan, the member information card should be included in the plan.

You will use this information in many ways as you learn to know and respond to each member individually. It helps to know about each member, especially if there is a medical emergency. In cases where neither of the parents nor a responsible family member attends the church, special education workers do well to have both an information sheet and a medical emergency form. A sample of the medical emergency form is given in the Appendix. Be certain the form includes information about the hospital preference, primary care physician, and where parents or caregivers can be reached while the member is in your care. Ask for important medical history of each member. Explain the information will be kept confidential and will be used only in an emergency.

What about a medical emergency plan?

Because of the types of physical impairments and medical conditions associated with mental retardation, a wise teacher will have a written medical emergency plan in place. Post the plan in a highly visible area with information files close by.

Keep these considerations in mind when you develop a medical emergency plan for your circumstances.

- Every teacher should be prepared to handle a medical emergency. Know first-aid and have CPR training. These classes are available through the American Red Cross, public school community-education classes, and local hospitals.
- Many of your members have a history of seizures, at times with respiratory arrest. Not all seizures come on in the same way. Find out what to look for and expect should the member go into a seizure.
- Keep a first-aid kit in the room. Restock it regularly.
- Decide which workers will handle first-aid, who will go for any needed help, who will call for an ambulance or professional medical services if necessary.
- If you teach alone, make plans with the teacher in an adjacent classroom to assist you in an emergency. If you do not have another teacher close by, ask for a telephone extension to your room or explain you will need another worker in the room with you.
- Teach members how to use the phone or go for help in an emergency. Post emergency phone numbers near the telephone or show members where they should go for help.
- In cases where you know that a member has a fragile health history, make certain a responsible worker is in the room at all times. Develop a clear communication system for seeking help in these cases.

Perhaps a trained medical professional goes to your church. Know where he or she is located during Sunday School. Inform the professional about the medical condition and get permission to notify him or her in case of an emergency.

We have one child in our church who is mentally handicapped. Why can't we put him with the special education adults during Sunday School?

Would you want your child to attend Sunday School with a group of adults?

The interests and activities of adults with mental disabilities are the same as those of their age-group peers. The interests and activities of a child with mental disabilities are the same as those of his age-group peers.

This discussion was handled with greater detail in the chapter on mainstreaming. We mention it again because this question or discussion is raised frequently.

It is not wise or best to place a child who is mentally handicapped in the same Sunday School department with mentally handicapped adults. Children should be taught with curriculum designed for the development and interests of children.

What curriculum needs to be used for adults who are mentally retarded?

Sunday School curriculum should be designed for the unique needs, interests, and abilities of mentally handicapped adults. Such a design excludes children's materials and simplified versions of youth or adult materials.

The best curriculum is one which is designed to teach the Bible to adults with mental handicaps so they can apply biblical truths to their lives. This type of curriculum assumes mentally retarded adults can learn biblical truths and that mentally retarded adults deserve the respect of being taught, rather than entertained, in Sunday School.

Appropriate Sunday School curriculum for adults with mental disabilities:

- has the Bible as its textbook.
- makes the Bible the center of everything taught in Sunday School.
- focuses on teaching goals, desired learning outcomes, the session emphasis, and the application of biblical truth to members' lives.
- contains activities, songs, and teaching procedures that are developed to help members realize one central biblical truth each session.
- encourages men and women with mental disabilities to know and love God, and at their level of understanding, to acknowledge Jesus Christ is the Savior.
- impacts and changes the lives of adults with mental disabilities for God's glory.

Explain the special education materials offered through the Sunday School Board.

During the past 10 years, we have seen the material grow.

It began as an attempt to provide for the high-interest, low-ability needs of mentally disabled adults by adapting printed materials designed for children. It has matured into a full-fledged, educationally sound set of materials designed and printed specifically for adults and older youth with mental handicaps.

Special Education Today[1] is designed for use by parents, teachers, family members, and church leaders who meet the special needs of persons with disabilities. The magazine includes:

- a forum for sharing ideas and success stories.
- music and recreation ideas.
- articles written about different types of disabilities.
- resource and church leadership information.

Special Education Teacher Packet[1] contains the resources teachers need to lead classes for adults or youth with mental handicaps. The packet includes:

- easy-to-use teaching procedures that allow teachers a flexibility in planning while reducing the amount of time spent each week in preparation.
- feature articles that focus on teacher development, family issues, ministry, and other subjects that support the teacher.
- colorful posters for visual aids and gameboards that can be used in large group or small groups.
- one copy of *Special Education Bible Study*.

Special Education Bible Study[1] is the quarterly member's magazine that includes:

- a biblical teaching picture for every Bible story.
- Bible stories written for low-level readers.
- activities to reinforce Bible truths for both reading and nonreading members.
- photos of mentally handicapped persons in each issue.
- real-life stories about issues and events familiar to members.
- activities to support and teach from real-life situations.
- activity pages to help members apply biblical truths to their lives.
- three unit songs.
- daily Bible readings.
- appropriate steps to becoming a Christian.

Special Education Cassette Recording[1] is an audiocassette which features the 12 unit songs suggested in the year's *Special Education Teacher Packets.*

Bible Discoverers Teaching Pictures, Bible Learners Teaching Pictures, and *Bible Searchers Teaching Pictures*[1] are a supplementary resources for special education Bible study curriculum. Each teaching picture set provides full-color teaching pictures of Bible stories or real-life situations with additional resources and helps printed on the back of each.

VBS Special Education Teaching Guide[1] provides for the teacher who wishes to offer a Vacation Bible School opportunity to persons with mental disabilities. The guide includes "How to Use This Book," theme interpretation, teaching plans for five two-hour sessions, and reproducible handouts. Art/craft, recreation, snack, and Bible learning suggestions are included.

What is an appropriate Bible translation for adults with mental disabilities?

These translations read on the 4th to 7th grade levels.
Good News Bible, The Bible in Today's English Version
Contemporary English Version
New Century Version
New Living Translation
New International Version
This Bible reads on a 3rd grade level and is said to be the lowest level full-translation version currently available.
New International Reader's Version

What are some suggestions for handling behavior problems?

Most behavior problems are caused because your members are confused or have too much stimuli bombarding them at once. Many potentially negative behaviors are avoided by well-prepared teachers and who have consistent teaching plans and teaching schedules.

Arrive before the first member.—Have an interesting activity ready, even if it is a structured social time. Begin each session with an activity that perks members' interests and makes them wonder, *What's next?*

Plan to teach individuals with activities adapted to the specific needs of your members.— Use visual aids, make eye contact, ask questions and give time for members to answer, and involve members in activities. Encourage members to respond to one another in appropriate ways. Stick with a regular schedule each week. When you do need to make changes, explain these to members in advance.

Know how to pace the session for your members.—Do not stay on one activity too long. Build in opportunities for members to move around and to talk purposefully. Short segments are a must for short attention spans.

Before you begin, have plans for how you are going to end the session.—Teach with an application and a closure in mind. Keep a smooth flow from one activity to another. If going from small groups to one large group and back to small groups causes too much distraction for your members, consider staying in one large group after you tell the Bible story. Suggestions in *Special Education Teaching Procedures* help you bring the session to a close.

The first thing to do in behavior management is to let members know the appropriate behaviors you expect from them. Display a chart of basic behavior expectations and review them on a regular basis. Make them general.

- Be respectful of others.
- Use materials appropriately.
- Work quietly.
- Remain in your assigned seat or area.
- Follow the directions of your teacher.

Give members concrete examples: "I talk to other members with a kind voice. I hold the

Bible carefully without tearing the pages. I use the markers when I write in my member's book. I stay in my chair or at the table until my teacher gives me permission to move. I listen to the teacher and do what she says."

Members lack self-control for a number of reasons. If you know that a member's behavior problem results from medication or a diagnosed syndrome, ask her caregivers and work trainers how they deal with the behavior. Be as consistent as possible with their way of handling the problem.

With other self-control issues, you can help members reduce the numbers of impulsive behaviors with firm and consistent expectations and clearly expressed consequences. In addition to the well-structured learning environment, be certain you give adequate supervision and plenty of praises for appropriate behaviors. "We are ready to hear a Bible story. Carl, I like the way you hold your Bible. Thank you, Annette, for helping Paula find the Scripture. William, you show us how to sit quietly and listen." A reminder is sometimes necessary when behavior appears to be heading for trouble. Members need to know there are specific consequence for each inappropriate behavior.

Gary did well the first two or three months in our department, but one Sunday he wandered toward the door while we were in large group. He said he felt sick; he needed to go home, so we took him. That happened for several weeks in a row. Finally one of our teachers, a supervisor at the work center, explained Gary had a history of that type of behavior at work. He liked to go home in the afternoons to watch his favorite TV shows. He tried to control the situation by saying he was going to vomit. If Gary left work early when he didn't have symptoms of being ill, he was put on down-time the next day without pay.

I talked with the house manager about the situation and agreed to follow the strategy used at home and work. On Sunday, I had a private conversation with Gary when he first arrived. I explained what I knew about his behavior history. No one was available to take him home during Sunday School that day. If he started to act fidgety, we would ask a teacher to take him for a walk and then come back to the room. If he complained of being sick that day, we would ask him to stay home the next week. Whether he came or not would be his decision to make. I asked Gary to repeat what I had said so I would be certain he understood. I announced to the entire department that the next week we would have our monthly birthday celebration. I knew Gary really enjoyed those celebrations.

Gary did well until just before time for the Bible story. Then he started to get out of his chair. The teacher touched him on the shoulder and asked him to go for a walk. Gary was quiet for just a few minutes when he came back. He complained of being sick. I reminded him of our earlier conversation and repeated that he would be making a decision about next week. He persisted, but we didn't take him home early.

I scheduled a meeting with Gary and his house manager that afternoon and explained what happened. The house manager agreed Gary had made the decision to stay home the next Sunday.

When Gary started to get on the van the next week, the house manager and our van driver reminded him of his decision the week before. Gary was angry and frustrated! But the consequence was great enough to motivate a change of behavior.

Give the member opportunity to express his anger or frustration before he loses control. One way to do this is to role play situations that create problems.

Why was there a conflict between Marla and Donna? It began 20 years before. Both high-functioning women wanted to be in charge at work, at home, at church. It was a classic case of power struggle. The women had so many arguments in Sunday School we began to do a series of role plays. Whenever Marla and Donna had a squabble, we would ask members to do an impromptu drama about ways to

settle it. We asked both women to take part in many of these. One hitch. They reversed roles; each played the other. I would like to say the women are good friends today. They aren't. But by learning to see the situation from each other's perspective, they have learned to control their conflicts.

Each individual needs plenty of loving acceptance.

Virgie loved coffee. She asked for it frequently: "Coffee-coffee-coffee." She asked for it as soon as she walked in the door each Sunday and several times throughout the morning. We began by giving her a red card and showing her a green card. We explained: "You keep the red card. We will trade a green card for the red when it is time for coffee. If you ask before we give you the green card, you will have to wait longer to get the coffee. After a few trials and errors, Virgie learned to wait for the green card and her coffee. We started out with three cups of coffee each session. With the card system, we were able to control the time span between cups until she only had one cup at the close of each session. Virgie learned not to ask for coffee all the time.

You want to help members learn to control specific behaviors. List those changes as goals. Work on one goal at a time. Plan strategies to help members accomplish those goals. Do not reinforce negative behavior by giving it too much attention. Before choosing a plan of action toward a negative behavior, honestly ask yourself if it is something you can ignore. Often praising and giving positive attention for appropriate behaviors are the best ways you can help members learn to avoid negative behaviors.

---

[1]Order these materials from Customer Service Service, 127 Ninth Avenue, North, Nashville, Tennessee 37234-0113; FAX (615) 251-5933; or e-mail to CompuServe ID 70423,2526.

[2]For more information about Glorieta Conference Center, call 1-800-797-4222: FAX, (505) 757-6149; or write, Glorieta Conference Center, Reservations Department, P.O. Box 8, Glorieta, NM 87535.

For more information about Ridgecrest Conference Center, call 1-800-588-7222: FAX, (704) 669-9721; or write, Ridgecrest Conference Center, Reservations Department, P.O. Box 128, Ridgecrest, NC 28770.

Q&A

Evaluate your current classroom.
• How can we make the most of the space we have?
• What are some practical ways we can increase storage and display areas?
• This is what we need to do about

walls _____

floors _____

lighting _____

How do you currently group department members? What changes do you need to make?

Write one thing you read about:
finding workers for your department _____

training teachers _____

planning meetings _____

Look at the sample Member Information Sheet. How would you adapt it for your department?

Develop a medical emergency plan for your current circumstances. List the steps:

1. _____

2. _____

3. _____

Evaluate your current Sunday School curriculum. Is it appropriate for your members' ages and skills abilities? Why?

List ways to avoid or manage behavior problems in your department or class.

1. _____

2. _____

3. _____

A Place for Beginning

A place for beginning:
- meets needs.
- begins with ministry.

Basis for Ministry

"The Spirit of the Lord is on me, because he has anointed me to preach good news to the poor. He has sent me to proclaim freedom for the prisoners and recovery of sight for the blind, to release the oppressed, to proclaim the year of the Lord's favor" (Luke 4:18-19, NIV).[1]

Jesus spoke these words in the synagogue in Nazareth. He was saying He had come to meet every human need. As Christians we need to follow Jesus' example and meet the needs round us. He included everyone in His ministry, and so should we if we are to follow His example. That means the church needs to be a place for everyone.

Persons with disabilities need to be cared for by church members. Not only do church members need to care for special-needs persons, but also we need to care for the families and caregivers of persons with disabilities. Special-needs persons and their families or caregivers make up about 94 percent of the population! That is a significant number of people who need to be part of the church family. Unfortunately we are not caring for anywhere near that number of persons.

Jesus said, "The harvest is plentiful but the workers are few. Ask the Lord of the harvest, therefore, to send out workers into his harvest field" (Matt. 9:37-38, NIV).

If Jesus has told us to meet needs, then why don't we do that with persons who are disabled? Several reasons might explain our reluctance to reach out to these persons:

- Fear.
- Uneasiness.
- Pity.
- Embarrassment.
- Hopelessness.
- Avoidance.

While these reactions may seem natural in some instances, they are excuses. If we are honest, we admit we don't really know how to relate to special-needs persons and their families. Therefore, we avoid them. We might be embarrassed and uneasy that we will say or do the wrong thing. We may feel the situation of the special-needs person is hopeless. This could lead to feeling pity for the person and the family. Perhaps we have never been around special-needs persons, and we are afraid of them because they may respond inappropriately, may have no control over their bodies, or may not understand us because of visual or hearing impairments.

Excuses are a real challenge to hurdle. Getting to know a special-needs person and his family can take away most fears and inhibitions you might have. These people are more like us than they are different from us. We can help provide them the spiritual support they need to face the difficulties that come their way. We can be a presence and provide a sense of hope. We can help to provide a place where they can use their unique gifts to serve God. We can care for them, and we can accept the contribution they have to offer to God's kingdom.

Steps to Beginning a Special Education Ministry

The desire to have the ministry may be the result of having special-needs persons as part of your church. Or you may not have a special-needs person in your church now, but you just want to be prepared for the time a family comes to your church with a special-needs person. In either case beginning a special education ministry requires preparation and planning. You might think of starting a ministry like taking a walk. Each step leads to the next step and so forth. Several steps are needed for beginning a special education ministry.

- Pray.
- Talk to the church staff.
- Establish a committee.
- Survey your church building.
- Survey your church members.
- Contact local agencies.
- Determine the ministry direction.
- Recruit and train teachers/volunteers.
- Remove physical, psychological, stereotypical, and theological barriers.
- Promote the ministry.
- Visit prospects.
- Begin the ministry.
- Evaluate.

Pray

After you have made a commitment to begin the ministry, the logical next step is to pray about the ministry. In your time talking to God, He will provide you direction and strength. Another source of seeking God's direction is to seek biblical insight. Read Bible passages about how Jesus ministered to people. Two passages are mentioned in this chapter. Look for others. Through prayer and Bible study you will have a strong foundation to begin the ministry.

Talk to the Church Staff

Having support from the church staff is important. Take time to include them in your vision for a special education ministry.

Before you can educate them, you must educate yourself. Do this in several ways. Talk to others who are involved in a special education ministry. They can provide practical insights about successes and failures. They can also be sources of support and encouragement as you venture out on this new undertaking. Other sources for information are books and magazine articles. Read as much as you can on the subject. You will not know everything, but you will be building a base of knowledge to which you can constantly add more information. Parents and caregivers of persons with special needs are an important source of information. Listen to them. Who better knows about the needs of a person with disabilities?

After you have acquired some information, then you will want to talk to the staff. They may have some experience with special-needs persons and their families, or they may be totally new to the ministry. Share information you have learned. Encourage them to support you and to be involved in this important ministry.

Many of the excuses mentioned earlier will be the reaction of church members. They need to be educated just as you and the staff have been educated. By educating church members before the ministry is begun, you may be able to alleviate some of their fears and uneasiness. Encourage them to be involved in the ministry by volunteering to help in small ways such as providing refreshments for socials, having a person with a disability sit with them during worship, and helping in special education Vacation Bible School.

Taking time to prepare the church—staff and members—can go a long way in helping the ministry get off to a good start.

Establish a Committee

You cannot work alone. You will need some help. A committee of interested persons can provide the support you need. Include a staff member as a committee member.

The committee needs to have the responsibility of establishing guidelines for the ministry.

This might include setting goals, finding out about health regulations, preparing a budget, securing teachers and doing a background check, making recommendations to the church, and so forth. The responsibilities of your committee will be based on your needs.

Survey Your Church Building

Survey your church to see if the facility is accessible for persons who are disabled. Persons who use wheelchairs will not come to the church that only has steps and no ramps. If the rest rooms will not accommodate wheelchairs, special-needs persons will find it hard to be at church for any length of time. In addition to ramps and rest rooms, check accessibility for parking, water fountains, doors, walkways, and worship.

If you have areas that need improvement, talk to the staff and the special education committee. They may have recommendations on how to handle the situations that need improvement. Observe the procedures your church uses to follow through with your recommendation. The recommendations may need to be discussed by the building and property committee, the deacons, and the finance committee.

Survey Your Church Members

How do you go about finding prospects for the new ministry? A good source is church members. They may have family members who will be prospects. They also may have friends, coworkers, and acquaintances who know a person who is disabled.

Survey the community around your church. Persons who are disabled likely are in the area. They will be prospects for your ministry if they do not attend church somewhere else.

Contact Local Agencies

Contact local agencies to see what services they provide. You may not want to duplicate something they are already doing. Also you will want to let them know your plans so they can refer prospects to you.

Also contact group homes and sheltered workshops in the community. Prospects abound in these settings.

Determine the Ministry Direction

Determine which ministry you will begin. Bible study is a good place to start. Coming to church on Sunday morning can be a treat for persons who are disabled. They are taught Bible truths and ways to apply what they learn to their everyday lives. By providing a place for the persons who are disabled, the family will have a time of respite and be able to participate in Bible study themselves.

In addition to Bible study, you might want to provide respite care for families so the caregivers can have some time away. This might be a time when a husband and wife go out to dinner or to a movie.

A friendship ministry would involve volunteers taking the person who is disabled out to shop or to lunch. This ministry can provide a blessing to both the disabled person and the volunteer.

Recruit and Train Teachers/Volunteers

Training may be provided through:
- qualified people in the community.
- local Baptist association.
- state Baptist convention.
- Sunday School Board of the Southern Baptist Convention.

• other churches.
Training will help teachers and volunteers feel more comfortable in new situations.

Remove Barriers
Barriers to remove include:
  • *physical barriers*.—Look at the accessibility survey you conducted. Remove as many barriers as you can. Some persons with disabilities will need transportation. Look into the possibility of providing for this need.
  • *psychological barriers*.—Help church members see the need for the ministry. Through the education process many will have a change in attitude toward persons with disabilities.
  • *stereotypical barriers*.—Often people have preconceived ideas about persons with special needs. Church members may think persons with mental disabilities cannot learn and cannot be active members of the church. This stereotype could not be further from the truth. Help church members identify stereotypes and then begin to break down that barrier.
  • *theological barriers*.—Persons with disabilities are like you and me. They have the ability to understand the plan of salvation and should have the opportunity to hear about God's love and free gift of grace and redemption. They have the ability to accept or reject the gospel. Persons with mental disabilities need to to know the love of God through Jesus Christ, too. Every person is a spiritual being with the potential for responding to God through a unique relationship with Him. Wholeness is the promise of the kingdom of God which may be received through faith in Jesus Christ. The church has the responsibility to give these individuals the opportunity to experience fullness, wholeness, and purposefulness.

Promote the Ministry
No one will know about the ministry unless you promote it. Some ways to do this are:
  • *letters*.—Send information to church members and identified prospects.
  • *advertisements/flyers*.—Post advertisements and flyers in prominent places such as grocery stores, restaurants, doctor's offices, and so forth after securing permission to do so.
  • *brochures*.—Include information in new member packets and to members so they can give the brochure to prospects.
  • *church newsletters*.—Include a column in each issue, highlighting activities.
  • *bulletin boards*.—Decorate a bulletin board to keep church members informed about activities, past and present.

Visit Prospects
Nothing can substitute for a personal visit to the prospect and his or her family. By being in the home setting, you will learn so much about the special-needs person. The parents can tell you about their family member. You can talk directly to the person who is mentally disabled. Coming to church will be less of a traumatic experience because the special-needs person will know you. Just by visiting you are showing an accepting attitude—that you are providing a place for everyone.

Begin the Ministry
If the ministry you choose to start is a department for persons with mental disabilities, prepare the room as discussed earlier and order Bible study materials to meet the needs of your members.
    The first Sunday members come to their new class will be an exciting day. All the planning and preparation will pay off as you begin the ministry. Look forward to many blessings as you teach and learn from your members.

If the ministry you begin is to provide opportunities for preschoolers, children, youth, and adults to be mainstreamed in Sunday School, make sure teachers and members are prepared before the person arrives.

If the ministry is respite care, provide training for volunteers. Become acquainted with the family for which you will provide the ministry.

Evaluate

No ministry would be complete without evaluation. Determine what works and what doesn't work. Make adjustments as needed. Know that what you are doing is important and has eternal consequences. For a separate Special Education Sunday School use the checkup in the Appendix. For mainstreaming special-needs persons use age-group checkups in the *Toward 2000* series books.

[1]From the Holy Bible, *New International Version*, copyright © 1973, 1978, 1984 by International Bible Society. Subsequent quotations are marked NIV.

List the steps to beginning a special education ministry.

1. _____

2. _____

3. _____

4. _____

5. _____

6. _____

7. _____

8. _____

9. _____

10. _____

11. _____

12. _____

13. _____

Are any steps more important than others? Discuss your answer.

How Accessible Is Your Church?

Use this survey to determine the openness and accessibility of your church.

More than 49 million people in the United States have some form of disability. This number includes children born with disabilities, people who have been involved in accidents, others who have developed debilitating diseases, and older people who have experienced decreased mobility or sensory perception.

Christians with disabilities need to continue to contribute to and enjoy the fellowship and support of the church. The following survey can be taken to determine how readily a person with a physical disability could participate in church activities.

PARKING SPACES

Yes No 1. Are accessible parking spaces close to the building?
Yes No 2. Are the spaces clearly marked by the International Wheelchair emblem?
Yes No 3. Are the parking spaces 12 1/2 feet wide?
Yes No 4. Is the area from the parking space paved even if the rest of the parking lot is unpaved?
Yes No 5. Is there curb-cut from the parking spaces to the walkway?
Yes No 6. Is it possible to get from a parked car to the inside of the building without going up or down a step or steps?

ENTRANCES / EXITS

Yes No Is at least one primary entrance to each building usable by individuals in wheelchairs?

WALKWAYS

Yes No 1. Are walkways at least 48 inches wide?
Yes No 2. Is the slope of walkways five percent or less?
Yes No 3. Are walkways a continuing common surface, uninterrupted by steps?
Yes No 4. Do walkways have a level 5-by-5 foot platform at the door that extends at least 1 foot beyond each side of the door?

RAMPS

Yes No 1. Do ramps have a slope no greater than a one-foot rise in 12 feet and a width of at least 36 inches?
Yes No 2. Do ramps have handrails on both sides, 32 inches above the surface?
Yes No 3. Do handrails extend 1 foot beyond the tops and bottoms of the ramps?
Yes No 4. Do ramps have nonslip surfaces?
Yes No 5. Do ramps have level platforms in front of doors that allow at least 5 feet of straight clearance?

DOORS

Yes No 1. Do doors have clear openings of 32 inches or more?
Yes No 2. Are doors operable with pressure (81 pounds or less) that could reasonably be expected from a disabled or frail person?
Yes No 3. Do doors with latch hardware have levers or other easy-grip handles?
Yes No 4. Is the maximum threshold for doorsills no more than 1/2 inch for interior doors and 3/4 inch for exterior doors?

REST ROOMS

Yes No 1. Is at least one accessible rest room on each floor?
Yes No 2. Does the entry door have at least a 32-inch clear opening?
Yes No 3. Do rest rooms have 5-by-5 foot turning space?
Yes No 4. Is at least one stall 36 inches wide with 48-inch clear depth from door closing to the front of the commode?
Yes No 5. Does the stall have a 32-inch wide door that swings out?
Yes No 6. Does the stall have grab bars on each side?
Yes No 7. Is there a wall-mounted sink with 29-inch clearance from the floor to the bottom of the sink?
Yes No 8. Are drain pipes and hot water pipes covered or insulated?
Yes No 9. Are faucet controls easy to operate?
Yes No 10. Are towel dispensers mounted no higher than 40 inches from the floor?

MULTISTORY BUILDINGS

Yes No 1. Is there an elevator to all levels of the building?
Yes No 2. Is the elevator door opening at least 36 inches wide?
Yes No 3. Is the elevator cab at least 51 inches by 68 inches?
Yes No 4. Are elevator controls 54 inches or less from the floor?
Yes No 5. Do stairs have handrails on both sides?

WATER FOUNTAINS

Yes No 1. Is at least one fountain on each floor accessible to people in wheelchairs?
Yes No 2. Is the fountain basin no higher than 30-36 inches from the floor?
Yes No 3. Are fountains operated easily by hand?

WORSHIP SPACE

Yes No 1. Are at least 2 seating spaces provided for wheelchair users? (Note: Some pews could be shortened by 36 inches to provide wheelchair space.)
Yes No 2. Is there wheelchair access to the choir?
Yes No 3. Is hearing amplification provided?
Yes No 4. Are large-print hymnals and Bibles available?
Yes No 5. Are bulletins designed with easy-to-read print?
Yes No 6. Does lighting prevent excessive glare and shadows on speakers and interpreters?
Yes No 7. Is the sanctuary adequately lighted to enable full participation?

WHAT NEXT?

1. Share the results of your survey with the congregation.
2. Evaluate your survey results.
3. Enlist a person with a physical disability to assist in setting priorities for improving the accessibility of your church.
4. Set goals and work through church structure to accomplish goals.
5. Publicize and celebrate each goal accomplished.
6. Publicize your church's accessibility to the community. Place the International Wheelchair Emblem in your newspaper and Yellow Pages ads, in brochures about your church, and on your church sign.
7. Welcome, minister with, and learn from all who come.

Adapted from *How Accessible Is Your Church?* by the North American Mission Board. Reprinted by The Sunday School Board with permission from the North American Mission Board, 4200 North Point Parkway, Alpharetta, GA 30202-4174.

Session Planning Sheet

Date: _____ Session Title: _____

Bible Passage: _____

Bible Truth: _____

Bible Verse : _____

Life Application: _____

Activity _____

Adaptation Idea _____

Materials Needed _____

Members in Group _____

Leader _____

Time Needed _____

Fellowship/Snacks _____

Create Learning Readiness 1. _____

                              2. _____

Guide Bible Study   1. _____

Apply Bible Truth to Life   2. _____

                              3. _____

                              4. _____

                              5. _____

                              6. _____

                              7. _____

                              8. _____

                              9. _____

                             10. _____

Close Session _____

Transition to Worship _____

Special Education Sunday School Checkup

As you plan and evaluate your ministry with this group, consider the following suggestions. Check each item you want to do. Add to or delete actions as appropriate for your church based on the church's mission.

On a regular basis (such as monthly or quarterly), use this checkup in meetings with leaders to check your progress toward desired results. Use a scale of 0–10, with 10 being excellent, to evaluate how well you feel you are doing in each area. Place your evaluation on the line to the right.

We Want to: Evaluation

1 Reach Mentally Retarded Persons and Their Families/Caregivers

- Set and work toward enrollment and attendance goals.   _____
- Enroll persons who are mentally retarded in Sunday School.   _____
- Enlist a leader who is coordinating and encouraging
  outreach efforts to persons who have mental retardation.   _____
- Participate in and enlist mentally retarded persons in
  prospect discovery activities.   _____
- Develop, maintain, and use a prospect file.   _____
- Participate in and involve members in regularly scheduled
  outreach visitation.   _____
- _____   _____
- _____   _____

2. Teach Mentally Retarded Persons the Bible

- Participate in the Sunday School Launch Event or conduct
  our own preparation to begin the Sunday School year.   _____
- Study the Bible as our textbook and use Special Education
  Sunday School literature published by the Baptist Sunday
  School Board.   _____
- Provide the best learning environment possible.   _____
- Provide at least one special Bible study
  opportunity at a time other than Sunday morning.   _____
- Practice total period teaching by providing one
  hour for Bible study each week.   _____
- Use an appropriate variety of teaching methods.   _____
- Encourage members to bring their Bibles to Sunday
  School and learn to use them in Bible study.   _____
- _____   _____
- _____   _____

3. Care for Mentally Retarded Persons and Their Families/Caregivers

- Maintain and use records and information on members and their families/caregivers, including ministry needs.   _____
- Assign each enrolled member and prospect to a teacher for ministry.   _____
- Pray regularly for members and their families/caregivers.   _____
- Provide or participate in ministry training for members and leaders.   _____
- Plan and implement actions to involve members in ministering to each other and prospects.   _____
- Conduct at least one parent-worker meeting each year.   _____
- _____   _____
- _____   _____

4. Witness to Mentally Retarded Persons and Their Families/Caregivers

- Participate in or provide evangelism training and encourage Christian members to witness.   _____
- Under the leadership of the Holy Spirit, witness to unsaved persons.   _____
- Enroll unsaved mentally retarded persons and encourage their participation in Bible study.   _____
- Teach the Bible to lay foundations for Christian conversion and spiritual growth.   _____
- As appropriate, teach evangelistically in Bible study sessions.   _____
- Develop and participate in activities designed to reach and cultivate unsaved persons.   _____
- Pray for family members/caregivers and mentally retarded person who have not yet made a profession of faith.   _____
- As needed, counsel parents, family members, and mentally retarded persons about Christian conversion and church membership.   _____
- Enlist mentally retarded persons who are Christian to join in witnessing to unsaved persons and winning them to Christ.   _____
- _____   _____
- _____   _____

5. Fellowship with Mentally Retarded Persons

- Affirm and recognize workers throughout the year and participate in a worker appreciation event. _____
- To nurture Christian friendships, plan and conduct social events for prospects and members. _____
- Provide parent-teacher fellowship opportunities. _____
- Provide family fellowship opportunities. _____
- Create a climate of trust and acceptance among members and prospects. _____
- Assimilate members and prospects through caring relationships.
- _____ _____
- _____ _____

6. Lead Mentally Retarded Persons to Worship

- Model consistent worship service attendance. _____
- Encourage members to attend the church's worship services. _____
- Encourage members to read the Bible, pray daily, and study Sunday School materials. _____
- Encourage members to participate in personal and family worship experiences. _____
- Engage the class in prayer ministries. _____
- _____ _____
- _____ _____

7. Administer

- Start additional classes and/or departments as needed. _____
- Enlist workers as needed and maintain recommended worker:pupil ratios. _____
- Provide and participate in basic and ongoing training. _____
- Participate in weekly or regularly scheduled planning and preparation. _____
- Begin Bible study groups beyond the Sunday School for unsaved mentally retarded persons. _____
- Use records to monitor enrollment and attendance. _____
- _____ _____
- _____ _____

TOTAL _____

Person/Family-Centered Plan

DATE: Oct. 8, 1997

DEACON: M. Smith

LAST NAME: Doe

ADDRESS: 1000 South Road

PHONE: 111-2323

PARENTS: (list Sunday School classes and other areas of involvement) John: teacher, boys 5th grade; choir; deacon (rotates off this year) Mary: member, Adult 5; ladies Bible study/craft class on Tuesday morning

CHILDREN: (list names, ages, Sunday School classes and other areas of involvement)
Adam: age 11, 5th grade class; RAs on Wednesday evenings
Seth: age 9, 3rd grade class; RAs
Stephen: age 5, preschool F; Mom's Day Out
Abby: age 9 months; preschool B

FOCUS AREAS FOR PLAN PERIOD Oct. 1997 TO Oct. 1998
- reaching/teaching
- ministry involvement
- integration
- building accessibility
- information sharing
- financial
- other:

RECOMMENDATIONS, INDIVIDUAL GOALS, STRATEGY:

1. Sunday School mainstream is not completely appropriate for Adam. Adam will attend age-grade class during large-group time for songs and the Bible story. Flo Beckett agrees to work one-on-one with Adam the first 30 minutes of that hour in a separate room. She will adapt activities for his skills, abilities.

2. Mary would like to sing in the choir on Sunday mornings. She needs someone to help with Adam during that time. Adam is not able to sit through the worship service. Four couples from Adult 5 agree to take turns once each month to provide extended session supervision. Adam will remain in the worship center the first 20 minutes (3-4 songs). He'll go outside or to the gym with a couple for recreation, a snack, then to B4 for a quiet Bible-related activity until worship dismisses.

3. Seth has displayed resentment toward Adam's disabilities for several months. He is currently receiving counseling. Adam should not be in the same Sunday School class with Seth. Promote Adam to 4th grade. Children's workers will provide separate opportunities for Adam and Seth at other times.

4. The Children's Ministry Council recommends starting a church-sponsored outreach to parents of youth with multiple disabiltiies for the purpose of providing support and information. John agrees to serve as an advisor for this project. Target date for the first meeting: February, 1998.

TEAM MEMBERS: (please sign)

_____   _____

_____   _____

_____   _____

_____   _____

Member Information Sheet

Name _____

Address _____

Phone _____ Age _____ Birthday _____

Name/Address/Phone of Parent/Caregiver _____

_____

Where to contact caregiver during Sunday School _____

_____

Physical disability? _____ Describe: _____

_____

Medical problems? _____ Describe: _____

Diabetes? _____ Allergies? _____ Food restrictions? _____

Describe medications _____

Special interests _____

_____

Day program (name and address of school, work program, daycare program): _____

_____

_____

Communication methods (verbal, reading, sign language, other): _____

_____

_____

_____

_____

Emergency Medical Authorization

Name _____

Date of birth _____

Address _____

City _____ State _____ Zip _____
In the event of an emergency,
I hereby give permission to _____
(name of church)

_____
(teacher's name or other adult sponsor)

to obtain medical assistance for the above mentioned person. I also give permission to the physician selected to hospitalize and
secure proper treatment for _____
(myself or ward—son, daughter)

Insurance Company _____

Address _____

Policy Number _____

My Social Security Number _____

Parent(s) S.S. Number _____ _____
(if appropriate)

Numbers where caretakers or family
can be reached: (*Please give name,* _____
relationship, phone)
_____

Allergies, medications, miscellaneous medical information: _____

_____

My primary-care physician and phone number: _____

Hospital preference (if in town): _____

Signature of person: _____

Signature of guardian (or parent) _____

Date: _____

*Check with your local agencies and/or a lawyer to determine if this form meets the requirements of your state laws.

DUTIES OF SPECIAL EDUCATION DEPARTMENT WORKERS

Department Director
- During Bible study activities, teach an individual or small group of persons who have mental retardation.
- Guide large-group time activities on Sunday morning.
- Secure literature and resources (if there is no secretary).
- Determine training needs and provide appropriate activities.
- Enlist all department workers.
- Represent the department on the Sunday School Council (if there is no division director).

Teacher
- During Bible study activities, teach an individual or small group of persons who have mental retardation.
- Reach out to find and enroll mentally retarded persons who need to be in Sunday School.
- Contact absentees weekly and all members in an assigned group regularly.
- Care for and minister to assigned members and their families/caregivers.
- Witness to members and their families/caregivers.
- Fellowship with members and their families/caregivers.
- Participate in regular planning.

Outreach-Evangelism Leader
- Lead department workers in evangelistic visitation and prospect discovery.
- Cooperate with the Sunday School outreach-evangelism director, as appropriate.
- Serve as a teacher.

Secretary
- Maintain department attendance records.
- Maintain department reaching contact records.
- Order literature and other supplies and resources.
- Serve as a teacher.

Division Director
- Design and be responsible for the budget in the Special Education Sunday School Division.
- Enlist all department directors.
- Provide training experiences for all workers.
- Participate in regular planning meetings.
- Plan to meet regularly with all Special Education Sunday School workers.
- Organize and maintain a resource system.
- Attend Sunday School Council meetings.
- Encourage all workers.
- Serve as a substitute teacher.

Disabilities Needs Assessment

Locating Persons with Disabilities In Your Church and Community

Your Church Leaders Want to Know How can we involve persons in our community who have physical or mental disabilities in the fellowship of our congregation?
Please help us by completing these questions.

1. Is a member of your family disabled? Yes _____ No _____

2. Do you have a friend or neighbor who is disabled? Yes _____ No _____

3. Describe the disability of your friend/relative. _____

_____

_____

4. Does he or she attend church regularly? Yes _____ No _____

5. If not, would he or she like to attend? Yes _____ No _____

6. Does your friend/relative need assistance with: (please check all that apply)
   Weekly shopping? _____ Transportation for medical appointments? _____

   Transportation to church?_____ Respite care? _____

   Medical equipment _____ Other? _____

7. We would like to include your friend / relative in church activities.
   Please give us the information below, or ask him or her to contact us.

Name _____

Address _____

City _____ State _____ ZIP_____

Phone _____

8. Do you have professional training in a field that would enable you
   to advise or assist in a ministry with persons with disabilities? Yes _____ No _____

9. What is your area of training or expertise? _____

_____

_____

_____

_____

_____

10. What experience have you had in working with persons with disabilities?

_____

_____

_____

_____

_____

_____

_____

_____

_____

11. Please give us information about yourself.

Name _____

Address _____

City _____ State _____ ZIP _____

Phone _____

Additional comments or suggestions for ministries: _____

_____

_____

_____

_____

_____

Teaching Methods and Activities

Art Activities
- cartoons/comic strips
- map
- poster
- drawing
- montage
- story mat
- collage
- mural
- sequence pictures

Art Tips:
- Use glue sticks or rolled tape rather than glue.
- Use colored pencils rather than crayons.
- Use colored chalk.
- Use modeling clay rather than play dough.
- Try water color pencils rather than Tempera™ paint.

Drama Activities
- acting out a Bible event
- contemporary skit and Bible parallel
- discussion starter
- monologue
- radio and TV format
- videotaping
- choral speaking
- dialogue
- interviews with dramatic personalities
- pantomime
- role playing

Music Activities
- group singing
- hymn text study
- recordings
- Autoharp
- hymn reading
- lyric writing
- rhythm instruments
- color-coded handbells

Paper and Pencil Activities
- creative writing
- puzzle (acrostic, crossword, word-search)
- quiz (definitions, fill-in-the-blanks, multiple- choice, matching, open-ended statements)
- chart
- worksheet

Personal Experience Activities
- outreach visitation
- personal witnessing
- ministry project (collecting food or clothes; care packages)
- nature walk

Learning Games
- Concentration™
- fishing
- ring toss
- relays
- tic-tac-toe
- bowling
- ball toss
- gameboards

Purpose: To train pastors, ministers of education, and/or Sunday School directors to begin a Special Education ministry or to strengthen an existing Special Education ministry.

Chapter 1
A Place for Reaching
(30 minutes)

Before the Session:

1. Prepare an overhead cel or poster with the following quotation: "All of us, including those with special education needs, combine to create the mosaic of a church family."

2. Make posters listing categories of persons with special needs.
- mentally handicapped
- physically disabled
- visually impaired or blind
- learning disabled
- hearing disabled or deaf
- multidisability
- behavior disordered
- exceptionally bright

3. Make assignment cards for three groups.
- How do you contact persons with special needs? In the community?
- How do you contact persons with special needs? In homes?
- How do you contact persons with special needs? In group homes?

During the Session:

1. Using the statement on the overhead cel or poster, discuss the importance of reaching persons with special needs.

2. Discuss the categories of persons with special needs. Note that all of these persons can and should be members in our churches.

3. Form three groups. Give each group an assignment about how to reach persons with special needs. Allow time for group discussion; then ask groups to report. Brainstorm other ideas not mentioned.

4. Conclude by saying:
A place for reaching means a place to plan and provide for persons with disabilities because . . .
- God loves them.
- Jesus ministered to them.
- Millions of people need to be part of the church.
- All other ministries can benefit.
- Persons with special needs minister to you.
- The rewards are positive.
- Such ministry is evangelistic.

Chapter 2
A Place for Teaching
(45 minutes)

Before the Session:

1. Make an overhead cel or poster listing the following information:
- A Positive Learning Environment
- Adapting Activities
- Age-appropriate Activities
- A Session Schedule
- Sign Language
- Teaching Methods

2. Make copies of "Teaching Methods and Activities" from Chapter 3.

During the Session:

1. Lecture concerning the major points in structuring a positive learning environment.

2. Address general adaptation principles and brainstorm ways to adapt activities and concepts.

3. Discuss age-appropriateness, relationship to the emphasis, and relevancy to what is going on in members' lives.

4. Review the elements of a session.
- Create Learning Readiness (5-10 minutes)
- Guide Bible Study (20-25 minutes)
- Apply Bible Truth to Life (15-20 minutes)
- Close Session (5 minutes)

5. Form groups. Using "Teaching Methods and Activities," ask each group to develop a Sunday morning session based on Luke 19:1-9, "Jesus Was a Friend." Provide time for groups to report how they would lead the Sunday morning session.

Chapter 3
A Place for Mainstreaming
(45 minutes)

Before the Session:

Prepare a poster or overhead cel with the following definition of mainstreaming. *Mainstreaming is placing eligible exceptional persons in the same class with their age-group peers for instructional and social reasons. Mainstreaming means a place in all church programs and ministries for eligible exceptional persons to benefit and serve along with their peers.*

During the Session:

1. Discuss the meaning of mainstreaming and explain when mainstreaming is best and when it is appropriate for a person to be in a separate department. Discuss some common problems with mainstreaming. Brainstorm some solutions to the problems.

2. Form groups to use the book to explain exceptional persons who can be mainstreamed. Then have participants explain how to make adaptations for mainstreaming. Use the following list of persons who can be mainstreamed. Allow groups time to report.
- Persons with visual impairments
- Persons with learning disabilities
- Persons with ADHD
- Persons with physical disabilities
- Persons who are gifted
- Persons with autism

Chapter 4
A Place for Caring
(30 minutes)

Before the Session:

1. Prepare an overhead cel or poster with what it means to minister: To minister means to help or serve others.

2. Prepare a listing handout.

Ways Persons with Disabilities Can Minister

_____
_____
_____
_____

Ways Persons with Disabilities Can Serve

_____
_____
_____
_____

During the Session:
1. Explain what it means to minister.
2. Allow participants time to complete the handout. Then have them share their responses.
3. Discuss ministry to families, to single-parent families, and to adoptive families.
4. Role-play a support group for parents who have children with disabilities.
5. Brainstorm ways families need financial help.
6. Explain what a *Person/Family Centered Plan* is. Allow participants time to look over the example plan in the book. Give time for questions and discussion.

Chapter 5
A Place for Witnessing
(30 minutes)
Before the Session:
1. Make posters or overhead cels with the words:
   • Sin
   • Punishment
   • Forgive
   • Sorry
   • Believe
2. Make banners with the following Scripture verses:
   • John 3:16
   • Romans 3:23
   • 1 Corinthians 15:3-4
   • John 3:6
   • 1 John 4:15
   • Matthew 28:19-20

During the Session:
1. Give definitions for the words related to salvation. Explain that persons with disabilities need to know about salvation and that many are able to make salvation decisions.
2. Have participants read the Bible verses.
3. Share the following parts of a personal testimony before sharing your personal testimony. Ask for volunteers to share their personal testimonies with the group.
   • My life before accepting Christ.
   • My life after accepting Christ.
   • What Christ is doing in my life today.

Chapter 6
A Place for Worshiping
(30 minutes)
Before the Session:
Prepare a poster with the words of Psalm 63:4.

During the Session:
1. Read Psalm 63:4.
2. Explain that God desires all persons to worship Him. Note that we can worship Him through: daily quiet time, prayer partners, thanks, and praise. Lead participants to take their Bibles and spend some time in a daily devotion. After they finish the individual quiet time, have them return to the group and sing a song of praise to God. Finally, form pairs and spend time in prayer. Explain how these elements of worship are important for all persons, including disabled persons.

Chapter 7
A Place for Fellowshiping
(30 minutes)
Before the Session:
Prepare an overhead cel or poster with the following: A place for fellowshipping is the place where we can get to know and be friends with people who share our love for Jesus Christ.
During the Session:
1. Brainstorm ways to fellowship with the following:
   • Individuals
   • Class
   • Department
   • Other departments
   • Other churches
2. Form groups and have each group plan a fellowship. Give time for each group to report.

Chapter 8
A Place for Organizing
(30 minutes)
Before the Session:
Write out the 16 questions found in Chapter 9—one question per sheet of paper.

During the Session:
Hand out the questions prepared before the session. Ask participants to find the corresponding answers in the book and report their findings. Brainstorm any additional information that pertains to each question.

Chapter 9
A Place for Beginning
(30 minutes)
Before the Session:
1. Prepare cutouts of shoe prints.
2. Have paper, scissors, felt-tip markers, and glue for participants to use.

During the Session:
1. As you discuss steps to beginning a special education ministry write the following on the cutouts.
   • Pray
   • Talk to the church staff
   • Establish a committee
   • Complete an accessibility survey of your church
   • Survey to discover people/needs
   • Contact local agencies
   • Determine the ministries to start with
   • Recruit and train teachers/volunteers
   • Remove physical, psychological, stereotypical, and theological barriers
       • Promote the ministry
       • Visit
       • Begin the ministry
       • Evaluate the ministry
2. Ask participants to prepare a brochure advertising the new special education ministry. Give time for participants to show their work.

CHRISTIAN GROWTH STUDY PLAN

Preparing Christians to Serve

In the **Christian Growth Study Plan** (formerly Church Study Course), this book *A Place for Everyone: A Guide for Special Education Bible Teaching-Reaching Ministry* is a resource for course credit in five Leadership and Skill Development diploma plans. To receive credit, read the book, complete the learning activities, show your work to your pastor, a staff member or church leader, then complete the following information. This page may be duplicated. Send the completed page to:

Christian Growth Study Plan
127 Ninth Avenue, North, MSN 117
Nashville, TN 37234-0117
FAX: (615)251-5067

For information about the Christian Growth Study Plan, refer to the current Christian Growth Study Plan Catalog. Your church office may have a copy. If not, request a free copy from the Christian Growth Study Plan office (615/251-2525).

COURSE CREDIT INFORMATION

Please check the appropriate box indicating the diploma you want to apply this credit. You may check more than one.

❑ **Special Education in Sunday School** (LS-0104)
❑ **Preschool Leadership** (LS-0014)
❑ **Children's Leadership** (LS-0022)
❑ **Youth Leadership** (LS-0026)
❑ **Adult Leadership** (LS-0035)

PARTICIPANT INFORMATION

Social Security Number	Personal CGSP Number*	Date of Birth
| |–| |–| | | |	| | |–| | | |–| | |	| |–| |–| |

Name (First, MI, Last)		Home Phone
❑ Mr. ❑ Miss		
❑ Mrs. ❑		| | |–| | | |–| |

Address (Street, Route, or P.O. Box)	City, State	Zip Code

CHURCH INFORMATION

Church Name

Address (Street, Route, or P.O. Box)	City, State	Zip Code

CHANGE REQUEST ONLY

❑ Former Name

❑ Former Address	City, State	Zip Code

❑ Former Church	City, State	Zip Code

Signature of Pastor, Conference Leader, or Other Church Leader	Date

*New participants are requested but not required to give SS# and date of birth. Existing participants, please give CGSP# when using SS# for the first time.
Thereafter, only one ID# is required. *Mail To:* Christian Growth Study Plan, 127 Ninth Ave., North, MSN 117, Nashville, TN 37234-0117.
Fax: (615)251-5067